Ministry and the Family of the Permanent Deacon

Dottie Mraz

THE LITURGICAL PRESS
Collegeville, Minnesota

Cover design by Ron Merriman

9   8   7   6   5   4   3   2   1

Library of Congress Cataloging-in-Publication Data

Mraz, Dottie, 1942–
    Ministry and the family of the permanent Deacon.
    1. Deacon—Catholic Church.   2. Catholic Church—
Clergy.   3. Clergymen's families.   I. Title.
BX1912.M78 1987   253'.2   87-11787
ISBN 0-8146-1566-X

Dedicated to my Lord
and to his Deacon Phil Mraz—
a man of faith and my knight in shining armor.

Contents

Foreword

At a lower level of the hierarchy are to be found deacons, who receive the imposition of hands "not unto the priesthood, but unto the ministry." For, strengthened by sacramental grace they are dedicated to the People of God, in conjunction with the bishop and his body of priests, in the service of the liturgy, of the Gospel and of works of charity. . . .

Since, however, the laws and customs of the Latin Church in force today in many areas render it difficult to fulfil these functions, which are so extremely necessary for the life of the Church, it will be possible in the future to restore the diaconate as a proper and permanent rank of the hierarchy. . . . with the approval of the Supreme Pontiff . . . it will be possible to confer this diaconal order even upon married men . . . .*

With these words, the Fathers of Vatican II reinstated the hierarchical order of deacon in the Latin Church. The apostles developed the order of deacon to fill their need for assistants in ministering to the People of God. They looked for men who were "acknowledged to be deeply spiritual and prudent" (Acts 6:3), whom they could appoint to the task. When good men were found, they were presented to

---

*See *Vatican Council II: The Conciliar and Post-Conciliar Documents*, volume 1, ed. Austin Flannery (Collegeville: The Liturgical Press, 1975) 387.

the apostles "who first prayed over them and then imposed hands on them" (Acts 6:6).

Ministry and the Family of the Permanent Deacon relates the story of how God called one young man to the diaconate in the Church of Cleveland in 1977. It is told to us through the words of his wife who captures within this book the development of a vocation, a call from God to service in the Church.

Philip Mraz prepared for the diaconate at a time when these formation programs were in the developmental stage. The author is able to lead the reader through Phil's preparation for orders because she lived this formation period with him. She shared his sacrifices, answered his questions, supported his weaknesses, acknowledged his strengths, and grew with him in faith.

The life of a pioneer is never easy and without difficulty. Dottie has a beautiful way of describing the growth she and her family experienced as their husband and father gave himself to a life of service to the Church of Cleveland. She describes the difficulties that arise in a family when a man must fulfill the responsibilities of two sacraments, Orders and marriage.

The reader will grow with this beautiful family as they prepare for ordination day and will struggle with them as the new deacon appears to be taken from their midst in his service to others. The deacon's wife is able to share the family's feelings and the solutions they discerned to the difficulties of this new life-style.

Dottie shares her joys and sorrows with the reader while relating how she lived her marriage vow to her husband, now an ordained deacon, "for better, for worse, for richer, for poorer, in sickness and in health, until death do us part."

Before I read a draft of this book, I thought that a wife's view of the diaconate would be of value only to permanent diaconate candidates and their families. But Dottie Mraz has handled the topic of ministry in such a way that this book will assist anyone who seeks a greater understanding of ministry in his or her life, whether as an ordained minister in the Church, a married person or parent, or as a single professional person. We all share through our Baptism the life of Christ, and his life is one of service to others.

Abbot Roger W. Gries, O.S.B.
Saint Andrew Abbey
Cleveland, Ohio

Preface

One afternoon, more than four years after my husband Phil had been ordained a deacon for the diocese of Cleveland, Ohio, I sat at my desk with pen in hand.

"Don't bother Mom; she's making her book," my ten-year-old son Bob scolded his brother as they came in from school.

"Really?" his brother asked. "Hey, Mom, the first sentence of a book is the most important!"

I could not help but smile; so far I had four sentences punctuated by sixteen interruptions.

Thus began the writing of this book, a book first conceived when Phil and I met with his five classmates and their wives a short time before the men were ordained as deacons in June 1977. We spent the evening get-together praying, reminiscing, and looking forward to a life of fuller service with a sense of joyful anticipation.

"Someone ought to write a book about all of this!" one of the wives exclaimed in her enthusiasm.

Although her words were not directed at me, I had the feeling they were somehow meant for me nonetheless.

In the months following Phil's ordination, my attitude of keeping my feelings about the program to myself gradually changed. Although sharing the reality of living the diaconate with individuals and groups was not always easy, there were numerous opportunities as well as much encouragement for me to do just that. Finally, nearly nine years after the word "diaconate" had entered my life and three months after Phil had been told he had terminal cancer, I began to write this book in earnest.

The story begins with Phil's first mention of the program, relates not only my personal diaconal journey but the diaconate's effects upon my marriage and family as well as our acceptance of the Lord's will, and concludes with my present experience as a deacon's widow.

My purpose in sharing the indescribable joy and sense of accomplishment as well as the pain and frustration of my experience is twofold. First, I hope that others who are interested in knowing more about this unique ministry will come to better understand what it means to be the supportive wife of an ordained deacon.

Second, it is my fervent prayer that this work will help to foster a more open sharing among those in diaconate programs everywhere because, eventually, I hope to see a full-time ministry—a ministry *by* those within the program *to* those within the program—become a worldwide reality.

Even though I have had little contact with those outside of our diocese, I am assured by those who have that, although each diocese's program is unique, the essence of what those in other diaconal communities have experienced is the same. Thus, I expect the majority of wives in the diaconate will be able to relate to much of what is within these pages, and many will be able to relate to most of it. I hope they will find comfort, as I have, in knowing that they are not alone, that there seem to be some "universal, normal, okay diaconate feelings," and that others have survived adjusting to a diaconal life-style and have actually grown remarkably in the process.

Despite the fact that it has been fifteen years since the diaconate made its quiet entrance into my life, I feel somewhat limited in what I have to share, for I am certain that much of what the diaconate is remains a mystery to me—so much a mystery that I doubt I will fully understand what my being a part of the diaconate and what its being a part of me really means until I have lived my life through. But I have the feeling that the one thing which will remain constant is that the diaconate will always be a special part of my life.

I look at the diaconate as God's gift to both Phil and me. The call, being open, the diaconate, ministry—these things are special, and I will always feel privileged to have had a share in this ministry of service to the People of God.

Part of my personal ministry has involved the writing of this book, and, with all creative work, one needs to give thanks. I begin with a thank you to my Lord, the author of all. I thank him for his numerous nudges to keep me aimed in the right direction. I thank him, too, for the gift of the seventeen years Phil and I shared, for our five beautiful children, and for the years we shared as a family united in, with, and through the diaconate.

I thank my husband Phil for his constant support and encouragement in all of my endeavors, but most especially for urging me to write and then making me promise to finish this project despite my numerous misgivings.

How could I not thank my children—Phil, Tom, Kathy, Bob, and Andy. Without their efforts and words of encouragement this project might never have been completed. My children deserve special thanks for their patience while I persevered in this project after Phil's death. Their generally uncomplaining attitude when suppers were late or rather hastily thrown together because I had allowed my writing to overflow its allotted time is most appreciated. I am also grateful for their editorial assistance which I found filled with amazing insight and understanding.

A special thank you goes to Sr. Judy Cole, C.S.J.; Rita Zayac; Elaine Wise; Beth Sinkovic; and my mother, Dorothy Claire—all of whom patiently, uncomplainingly, and repeatedly read the manuscript.

Many others have also given generously of their time and talents. Although they are too numerous to mention here, they know who they are and I thank them. To each and every person who has helped, supported, or encouraged me in my writing in any way I say, "Rejoice with me now. The book is finished. Thank you and I love you."

Dottie Mraz

1

Answering the Call

"**H**ey, Honey, look at this! They're ordaining a married man to something called the 'diaconate.' While he is living the life of a layman with his wife and children, he will be sharing in a ministry of service as an ordained deacon, a member of the clergy." From across the room, my husband Phil showed me the article in our diocesan newspaper, the *Catholic Universe Bulletin*.

"That's nice," I said as I carefully lowered my pregnant frame into our comfortable high-backed rocker.

I had always been a believer in men taking an active interest in their faith, so it was good to see Phil reading the *U.B.* and to hear his interest in the new developments within the Church like this "diaconate," whatever it was.

"Listen to this! Not only will he perform works of service within his own parish or church community, but he will also be helping with all types of liturgical services."

"That's nice," I replied as I reluctantly gave up my comfortable chair and returned to the kitchen to finish preparing supper.

Thus passed my first encounter with the diaconate. There certainly was nothing very earthshaking about it.

One night a few weeks later, Phil came home late from

work. He stood on the landing just inside our back door sheepishly holding something behind his back.

"How would you like to be married to a deacon?" he asked.

"Okay, as long as that deacon is you!" I teased as I gave him a quick welcome-home kiss and then returned to stirring the beef stew.

"Guess what I did!" he continued unaffected by my casual manner. "I stopped at the chancery and picked up some information on the diaconate. I brought an application too." Phil was not joking. A booklet on the diaconate and an application were what he had been holding behind his back.

"Whatever prompted him to ask for information on this new program?" I wondered. Still, I did not take his interest seriously. Neither of us had ever been very adventuresome, so why should we get involved with something in the Church as new as the diaconate was in 1972? Maybe Phil would read the booklet and look over the application, but both would undoubtedly end up gathering dust on his dresser along with his other papers and "things to do."

Time passed, and God blessed us with another healthy son. We were now the proud parents of four children— Philip, who was almost six years old; Tom, four; Kathy, two and one-half; and our newborn, Bob.

Although our life was already busy, for some reason Phil seemed to feel drawn to the diaconate. Having neither the time nor the inclination to look over the information about the program, I asked Phil to tell me more about it.

"Deacons were an important part of the early Church," he said. "The institution of the diaconate was reinstated by the Second Vatican Council."

So this was not something new after all, only a recalling of something that had been valuable centuries ago.

"A deacon is a man of faith called by God to minister to his people by living a life of service. He also assists at liturgies, preaches, baptizes, prepares couples for marriage, officiates at weddings and funerals, and serves in many other ways. He is ordained by the bishop of his diocese and is directly responsible to him. A deacon is generally assigned to his home parish or to one nearby. He teaches the Catholic faith twenty-four hours a day through his words and actions. His family and secular work come first; then he uses his free time to work for the Lord.''

What Phil was describing would have to include a deep commitment on both our parts. Was I ready for that kind of undertaking?

''It is often called the 'permanent diaconate' to distinguish it from the 'transitional diaconate' to which seminarians studying for the priesthood are ordained,'' my husband continued.

'' 'Permanent' diaconate,'' I thought to myself, ''not 'temporary see how it goes,' but *permanent*.''

For three years, we had been involved in Christian Family Movement and our parish renewal program. These activities had been good for us, but the diaconate would not be like them. We were free to give up our present involvements at any time; the diaconate would be for the rest of our lives.

''If a deacon's wife dies, he may not remarry,'' Phil continued.

Why not? How could a man possibly continue a diaconal ministry with a house full of young children each constantly needing his undivided attention? How would Phil ever manage without a wife? That continued to bother me. I wanted my children to have a mother in their lives, even if I did not live to raise them myself.

''They are setting up a course of study for diaconate candidates at St. Mary Seminary,'' Phil continued.

How would my husband handle courses taught at a seminary by full-fledged professors? Even if Phil did well with the required studies, how would my rather quiet, shy husband ever be able to assist at liturgies or preach in a church filled with people?

There were so many unanswered questions. The diaconate would mean a lifetime of Phil's ministering to others in addition to his being husband, father, and electrician. What would ordination mean for me and the children? Could our family handle all the extra activity this program was certain to bring into our lives?

However, as my husband spoke, I sensed an excitement within him, and an unexplainable excitement began to grow within me, too.

For months, we thought and talked so much about the diaconate that applying was naturally the next step. Phil took charge of all the paperwork and telephone calls. In addition to an autobiographical sketch of his life and his family, my husband had to complete an application form covering all the usual basic information. He contacted his schools, asking that his records be sent to the director of the program. In addition, he obtained new copies of each of his sacramental records from the parishes where each sacrament had been received. There were also three letters of recommendation required—one of them from our pastor.

All I had to do was write a letter stating my willingness to become a part of the diaconate program, too. That I did one sunny Saturday afternoon while Phil watched the children. Somehow, in the process of applying, my apprehensions had melted away. If God were truly calling Phil to the diaconate, we would be accepted into the program, and if we were not being called by our heavenly Father, he would let us know in some way that the program was not for us.

There was a peace in trusting the Lord to lead us, a calmness in waiting to see what he had in mind for us, and a willingness to discover what the diaconate was to mean for us as we went along. Since I am a worrier by nature, achieving that sense of inner peace marked a big step forward in my personal relationship with the Lord. Phil may have been the one who was applying for admission to the diaconate, but I was growing already.

Submitting the required information was the first step in our being accepted into the program. The second step, if it could be called that, was waiting six months to hear from Fr. Bob Pfeiffer, the priest heading our diocesan diaconate staff at the time.

Finally, right before Thanksgiving, Father Bob telephoned. "I'd like to meet with you," he told Phil. "Would you be able to come to Saint Mary Seminary sometime soon?"

"Sure, I'd be glad to," I heard Phil reply. "I could stop some evening on my way home from work if that would be okay with you."

Thus, the first interview was arranged, and despite my objections to his wearing his work clothes for such an important event, Phil appeared at the seminary as he was— husband, father, electrician all in one package—to interview for a whole new way of life.

From what my husband shared following his meeting with Father Bob, I gathered things had gone well. We and the children were invited to the diaconate Christmas party to be held at the seminary a couple of weeks later. Following that, there would be a series of interviews for our whole family.

Oh, no! Our family at the seminary? Me being interviewed? How should I act? What should I wear? Could I fit the picture of what Father Bob and the staff thought I should be? What should a deacon's wife be like, anyway? How could I possibly know; I had never known one.

Trying to decide what a deacon's wife "should" be and thinking about trying to become whatever I thought the staff would expect me to be was making me very nervous. I knew I could never pretend to be something I was not without living a lie, and living a lie would never be for me. I became determined to be me, just me, and then wait patiently to see what would happen.

At the proper time, on the Sunday afternoon of the party, our family stood on the front steps of Saint Mary Seminary ringing the doorbell. The gentleman who answered politely ushered us to the dining hall where we were greeted with genuine warmth by those already gathered there. Father Bob promptly introduced us to the other two diaconate staff members, three ordained deacons, three men who were in formation, four who were going through the interviewing process, and all of their families.

Surprisingly enough, the deacons themselves did not seem to be anything special; they and their families seemed to be normal, everyday people. At least, there were no halos visible around their heads. It was obvious that each man and his family were different from all the others.

In addition to the friendliness and the variety of the people in the program, I was impressed by the excitement in the air. It was the same excitement which had filled us when Phil and I had thought or talked about the diaconate.

The next step for acceptance into the formation program was having two interviews in our home. Father Bob and staff member Josephine Jendrisak, a psychiatric social worker, each visited our family on separate occasions. Although I did not realize it at the time, they were not just there to talk about the diaconate. They needed to be sure that our family relationships were stable. Apparently the visits went well because, soon after, Phil and I were invited for an interview at the seminary with the third staff member, Fr. Ernie Hepner, a priest psychologist.

The evening of the interview, Father took Phil into his apartment to talk with him while I waited in the seminary lounge. When it was my turn, Father Ernie made polite conversation as we walked to his living room where I perched nervously on the edge of the sofa facing him.

"What do you see the diaconate as?" he asked me.

"Living a life of fuller service."

"What do you see as your role as the wife of a married deacon?" he continued.

"I would be Phil's helpmate and support him in his ministry in all the ways I could. But my main concern would be to keep things running smoothly at home. Then Phil would be freer to minister to others as he felt called." These were things I had carefully considered during the past few months, so the answers came easily.

After several more questions, my interview was completed, and we returned to the lounge to get Phil. Father Ernie interviewed us together while he walked us to the door as we left for home.

Not long after that interview, Father Bob informed us that Phil was to begin studies in January. We were finally on our way to discovering more about the diaconate, Phil by participating in classes and our whole family by taking part in the activities provided during our time spent in formation.

2

Formation

Any new experience Phil and I had undertaken in the past—like our marriage, having children, or owning a home—had many facets. The same was true of our diaconal experience, for in addition to classes, there were new friends, meetings, various social get-togethers, retreats, a family formation program, special liturgies, and evaluations. Each facet of the formation program had its own important role in preparing us for a lifetime of ministry.

The one thing we had expected from the first was that Phil and his classmates would have to study. Their intellectual preparation began with three-hour classes held twice a week during the regular school year. The subject matter presented in the sessions was much the same as that presented to the seminarians studying for the priesthood, but naturally, in two classes a week, the information could not be presented in quite the same depth.

The men seemed to find the classes interesting, enjoyable, and challenging with much assigned reading as well as occasional papers, projects, practice homilies, and final exams.

We wives were welcome to attend classes with our husbands whenever we could. Although some of the wives were able to do that regularly, it was impossible for me to manage. I was needed at home. At the same time, I really wanted to know what Phil was learning, probably because I had a vision of my husband coming out of formation a transformed person with knowledge far superior to mine and of us eventually reaching the point where I would no longer be able to carry on an intelligent conversation with my own husband. That was not the way I wanted the diaconate to be for us.

The solution to the dreadful dilemma of my daydreams was simple. Phil took a small tape recorder to class, and by listening to the tapes, I became familiar with his studies of theology, morality, the sacraments, marriage and canon law, Christology, the Christian Church, homiletics, and adult religious-education programs. Quite some curriculum for a young wife and mother!

Only twice in all the time Phil studied at the seminary was I able to attend classes with him. Being right there with the men and meeting the professors was good, for it gave me a taste of their personalities and made the taped classes more interesting and alive for me.

It was in other aspects of his studies that I became more involved. When there was a report or a project to do, Phil would discuss his ideas with me and ask for my comments. I would listen, make suggestions, and look over the finished product before he handed it in. When there was a homily to prepare, he carefully researched the readings for the day and checked his homiletic sources for comments. Here I helped again by making suggestions and listening to him practice the finished product.

After meeting the men in Phil's class, no one could possibly have said that a certain type of man was being called to the diaconate in Cleveland. Some were rather quiet and shy—at first. Others were outgoing and seemed very self-assured. Not only were their personalities very different, but their life-styles also varied widely. One of the men lived in Cleveland, while the others were scattered throughout the suburbs—two living in almost rural areas. Their secular occupations varied just as much. The class consisted of a photographer in the printing industry, a supervisor at a Ford Motor Company stamping plant, a doctor, a policeman, and my construction-worker husband. Six months later, a plant-maintenance engineer, who had begun his diaconate studies in another diocese, joined the class. This man had been born and raised in Hungary.

All six were married men. And just as each of the men was unique, so were each of the wives and families. Two of the wives had been born and raised in Europe—one in Hungary, the other in Germany. The number of children in the families ranged from two to seven, but, unlike us, some of the couples had offspring who were already grown and on their own.

Three men who had previously begun their diaconal studies individually at local Catholic colleges also attended classes at the seminary. Each fall thereafter a new class of men became a part of the program, too. As the number of men grew, so did the range of personalities and professions. However, as diverse as the men and their backgrounds were, we soon discovered that the one thing they had in common was their deep commitment to doing the Lord's work.

An unexpected benefit of being part of the diaconate was the opportunity for building community among us, which began with classes and continued with the monthly business meetings for diaconate couples at the seminary and with occasional get-togethers for the wives and families.

The purpose of one of the first ladies' meetings was for those of us new to the program to meet the wives of the three men already ordained and actively ministering. Very quickly, we saw that Dorothy, Effie, and Reneé were quite different from each other in appearance, age, personality, life-style, and church involvement.

The mother of two elementary-school children, Dorothy Newman was working full time as a guidance counselor for the Cleveland public schools. When asked about her involvement in her husband Joe's ministry, Dorothy told us she helped him very little and, in fact, seldom went with him when he was assisting the bishop or ministering in other parishes. This wife felt she helped her deacon husband most effectively by keeping things running smoothly at home.

Effie Johnson told us that four of her five children were grown and out of school and that she ran her own business, a beauty shop. Her husband Charlie's ministry assignment included his being the director of the Church-supported Martin de Porres Center in Cleveland's inner city where Effie aided him in whatever ways she could. Because they were a black couple in a diocese largely white, Effie told us that, until she could see the people had accepted him, her support of her husband's ministry included accompanying Charlie to the parishes he visited with the bishop so that he would not be the only black there.

Reneé Bals, about my age, supported her husband Jerry's ministry by taking care of their five children aged four months to eight years. She and her husband were so busy that getting a babysitter so they could attend a Church function together and go out for dinner afterwards was one way of giving them some time alone. I knew the feeling, and Phil was not even ordained yet.

"I remember when we were going to attend our first diaconate conference at Collegeville, Minnesota," Reneé related. "I didn't know what to wear. Then I decided I had to be me and just wore what I already owned."

"Hooray!" I thought to myself. "Thank goodness I'm not the only one who was uncertain what would be appropriate to wear to a diaconate function." I also now knew that I was not alone in my struggle to reach the decision to allow myself the freedom to be "me."

At the meeting that night I not only learned more about what it would mean to be the wife of an ordained clergyman in the Catholic Church, but I also found that, just as

I had suspected, there was no set mold for a deacon's wife and no set pattern for her life to follow. Through their sharing, these three wives helped me feel at ease with being a part of the program. I realized that they too were human, and, just as importantly, that each of them had been able to retain her individuality in spite of her husband's ordination and ministry.

Those of us in the program grew closer at social times, too, when we were able to have fun while becoming better acquainted with each other, the seminarians (the future priests of the diocese with whom the deacons would be working closely), and the seminary faculty. In addition, during the final year of formation, Phil's class met regularly as couples to pray, to share experiences, and to enjoy some social time together. Occasionally, Phil and I would meet with another diaconate couple just to relax and share our thoughts as well as prayer. We were finding that, outside of those in the diaconate, no one seemed to fully understand what we were about. Thus, those of us within the program were becoming more and more a source of strength and support for each other. Eventually, we formed a special, close-knit community.

Of course, the children were not left out of this community. At the end of our second year in the program, all of the families were required to take part in what was called a family formation weekend. Beginning with activities designed to discover who we were as individuals and working into each family's discussion of their own life-style and communication, the weekend ended with group experiences in communication and sharing.

As a follow-up to the weekend, each family became part of what is known as a family cluster.* Meeting regularly, cluster groups generally shared a meal, an enrichment activity, and relaxed, spirit-lifting conversation for the adults and informal play for the children.

*See Margaret M. Sawin, *Family Enrichment with Family Clusters* (Valley Forge, Penn.: Judson Press, 1979).

In addition the annual diaconate Christmas party, a summer picnic, and other activities afforded our youngsters an opportunity to meet the others in the program and to build lasting friendships. One of my growing fears was that the deacons' children would have unreasonable expectations placed upon them merely because their fathers were ordained clergy. I had heard about ministers' children having that problem and definitely did not want that for our young ones. I hoped that building friendships among these diaconal families would give our offspring peers who would understand their parents' commitment to ministry within the Church. At least they would have friends to talk with about being "deacon's kids" if they should ever feel the need.

Not only was the formation program itself designed to help us build a loving community relationship with the others, but it was also designed to help each of us get to know our God by building a deeper, more loving community relationship with him—Father, Son, and Holy Spirit. The classes and liturgies just naturally aided our spiritual growth. These regularly scheduled happenings became so much a part of our lives that the growth that came from them was practically painless.

Beyond that, all of the men and women in the program were encouraged to have a spiritual director and a regular confessor with whom they were to meet frequently. Although this idea was new to me, it proved to be very beneficial. When Phil and I first discovered that we were beginning to feel overly busy, Fr. Dave Fallon, Phil's spiritual director at the time, was the one who asked us both to write down what we were doing each day for one full week. I was nervous when Father Dave stopped at our home to see what we had discovered about our lives, for it was embarrassing to have to admit to him, to Phil, and to myself that I was spending little time in quiet prayer and had virtually no time for myself. Phil was doing a little better; at least he was attending daily Mass frequently and playing tennis occasionally.

At that time, my husband and I also became aware of the fact that since the diaconate had entered our lives, we had little time alone together. I could not help but think that perhaps being a part of the diaconate program was not such a good idea for us at this time. Fortunately, though, it was not necessary to leave the program because becoming aware of what was going on in our lives allowed Phil and me to work together at making the changes necessary for a more reasonable family life-style.

Each fall the program provided our spiritual growth with a not-so-gentle nudge in the right direction. It was then that all of the candidates and their wives attended a retreat planned especially for them. Although these annual retreats were intended as spiritual get aways, the conversation there generally centered around our respective families, ministry, and diaconate events and ceremonies.

The ceremonies were milestones on the road to ordination. Phil and his classmates were installed first as candidates. Their installations as lectors and then as acolytes followed respectively.

At the time of the candidacy ceremony, our parish bulletin included an announcement of Phil's installation. Although we had already begun sharing news of our commitment with a few close friends, this was the first full-fledged public declaration of our intentions. Notification of the ceremonies was also made in our diocesan newspaper along with an explanation of the diaconate program. Our whole diocese was learning about the diaconate right along with us.

One thing was certain; the diaconate had added a new dimension to our lives, a dimension which seemed to be causing such a busy family life-style that it was often difficult to fit everything in and keep our priorities in mind: family first, then Phil's secular work, and diaconate last. Although this sequence had often been preached by the staff, there were many times when we felt that the diaconate almost had to come first in order for us to stay in the program. As the diaconate claimed more and more of our time and energy, Phil and I were both seen less and less at our parish. We had no choice but to give up our former church involvements to make room for Phil's studies and the various programs and events.

But the diaconate was not the only thing complicating our lives; in November of Phil's second year of studies, our fifth child, a son named Andrew, was born. At the same time, construction in the greater Cleveland area was down, and Phil was laid off from work several times. Surprisingly enough, the layoffs were not all bad because they provided us with much needed time—time for us, time for our family, time to do some of the things we had been wanting to do around the house, and more time for Phil's studies.

Each spring, the diaconate couples were asked to evaluate how they were managing with the added dimension of the diaconate. Phil and I prepared for our annual interviews by asking ourselves some important questions and by openly discussing just how we felt. How was the program fitting into our lives? Or was it that our lives were fitting into the program? How were we as a family accepting this additional challenge? When Phil and I met with the diaconate staff at the seminary, we shared the results of our introspection as well as the frank discussions we had had before coming for the evaluation meeting.

Diaconal ordination was a goal for the future—something which Phil and I were working toward together. It seemed that this working together was good for us and was helping to make our marriage and our family even stronger. We knew it. The staff sensed this in us and told us so.

The first half of our last year in preparation for ordination was the same as far as our working together was concerned. However, during the final six months of formation, under the watchful eye of our pastor, Phil sampled many of the avenues of service available in our home parish and in Christian Family Movement. This expanded ministry involvement was quite a change from the regularly scheduled two classes a week to which our family had become accustomed. We had slipped rather easily into that routine, but this new one was a different story. Since there was no longer a planned schedule for us to follow, it became necessary for us to take charge of our own planning. But, because there were so many areas of ministry to be sampled and there was so much work which needed to be done, over-scheduling was always a temptation.

It was a busy time for Phil. Sometimes he was gone as many as three or four nights a week. That was just too much time away from home as far as I was concerned, because I found that I was often left home alone with the children— sometimes more often than I would have liked to have been. For me, this was the most difficult part of formation. But ministering to others was good for Phil, and the works in which he was involved helped him to get a better idea of the areas in which he could best serve. He was also developing a deeper confidence in himself and in the ever-growing feeling that he was indeed being called to ordained service. How could I possibly complain about his being gone so much! Yet, I knew some resentment was creeping into my life and signs of strain were entering our relationship.

"How do you feel about being the wife of an ordained deacon now?" the staff asked me at our final interview.

"Okay," I replied. "But you might as well know how I feel about Phil's being gone a lot," I told them. "He can be out one or two nights a week, but no more than that because I need my night out, too, you know. And sometimes we should both be home with the children. Our family time is very important."

Fr. Ernie Hepner looked troubled. "No more than one or two nights? What if an emergency comes up? You won't make *any* exceptions?"

"Exceptions, sure," I smiled. "But Phil can't schedule himself at church every night. After all, the children and

I need him, too. We are his *first* commitment. Besides, it wouldn't look good to have a deacon who believes so strongly in marriage and family with no time for his own family, would it?''

Father Ernie relaxed visibly. ''Okay,'' he said.

From the tone of that final interview, it sounded as though the staff expected Phil to be ordained. Now it was a matter of waiting to know for sure that he had been chosen for ordination as a deacon for the Church of Cleveland.

3

Preparing for Ordination

My first exposure to a diaconate ordination was at one of the monthly diaconate meetings where we viewed a movie of Deacon Charlie Johnson's ordination Mass. As I sat and watched the ceremony taking place in front of me, I could not help being fascinated and a little frightened by the awesomeness of what I saw. What really surprised me was the fact that Charlie prostrated himself before the altar while the Litany of the Saints was sung. I had never seen anything like this before and was embarrassed at the thought of Phil's doing the same thing with our family and friends present.

Viewing the movie was exciting, but at the same time, it left no doubt in my mind about the seriousness of our diaconate involvement. At his ordination Phil would be standing before God and God's people, dedicating his life to the service of the Church. Although I would not be ordained, I would be dedicating my life to that same service.

Halfway through their final year of formation, even before their last interviews and their letters from the bishop stating their acceptance for ordination had arrived, Phil and his classmates were told to begin planning for their diaconal ordination.

Just as making plans for our wedding had indicated the final commitment Phil and I were making to each other, preparing for ordination required us, together, to make a similar final commitment to ministry within the framework of the Church. This called for discerning, once and presumably for all, that Phil's call was truly from God. As I remember it, my husband and I suffered together through a good case of pre-ordination jitters similar to those we had experienced before our wedding day.

There were many questions to be answered. Was Phil really being called to a lifetime ordained ministry? If he was being called, then, as his wife, I was being called, too, but in a different way. The diaconate had already changed our lives and seemed to promise to continue to do so. Was this what God wanted for us? Was it what we wanted for ourselves? After considerable soul-searching, Phil and I were eventually able to reach a mutual decision.

Time itself had provided us with our first clue as to what decision was right for us, for the longer we had been in the program, the more comfortable we had become with being a part of it. In addition, Phil had done well in his studies, and because ministry itself had proved exciting and rewarding for both of us, we felt good about a lifetime commitment to the diaconate. Not only that, but friends in our parish and others in the program had often supported us during the formation years by remarking that they felt Phil had a special calling. Even the diaconate staff had had good things to say about us; they seemed to be confident that Phil's call was indeed from the Lord.

All of these signs we took as confirmation of our own inner feelings that God himself had chosen Phil, me, and our family to be a part of the diaconate, and we decided that, unless some insurmountable obstacles were placed in our way, Phil would petition for ordination. This he did by writing a formal letter to Bishop James A. Hickey of Cleveland. Knowing that thus far the diaconate had been good for our whole family, the children and I composed a letter stating our willingness to be a part of Phil's lifetime ministry. The letter was not a requirement but rather a reaffirmation of our own personal commitment. We all signed the letter; even our baby, Andy, made his mark on the page.

Then, in addition to our final interview with the diaconate staff, Phil met with the director of clergy personnel. Together, they decided Phil's pastoral ministry assignment following ordination was to be the deacon for our home parish with the emphasis of that service in the area of family programs and concerns as well as ministry to the Christian Family Movement groups within our diocese. It was a logical choice as these were the areas which seemed to have interested Phil most during the time when he had sampled various types of ministry.

Not long after this decision, Phil and I had our final interview. This one was with Bishop Hickey. Although I had met the bishop several times on previous occasions, none had been as important as this meeting. The discussion we shared centered on the diaconate, the diocese, our family, and the ministry which Phil would be performing following his ordination. All the while, our bishop gently questioned us in order to learn all he needed to know before he could accept Phil's petition and ordain him a deacon.

As the interview progressed, I was surprised to find that, as nervous as I was, it seemed right for Phil and me to be there. "Yes, Lord," I thought with joyful confidence, "I am certain you have called our family to the diaconate."

Bishop Hickey's letter accepting Phil's petition for ordination arrived two months before the ordination. It was now simply a matter of Phil's finishing his pastoral ministry training and of our planning for the day when he would become a member of the clergy of the diocese.

Just as our final soul-searching in preparation for ordination had been much like that before our marriage, our ordination preparations included plans similar to those we had made for our wedding. This time, however, there were six men and their wives involved. Here, frequent meetings were added to already busy schedules.

All things considered, the preparations moved along without any earthshaking complications. One man had taken charge of ordering formal invitations in the design the class had chosen; someone else volunteered to mail them to all who were on the protocol list. Another of the men arranged for six matching stoles and dalmatics to be made. (A dalmatic is a vestment similar to a chasuble worn by a priest at Mass except that the side seams of a dalmatic are sewn closed to form sleeves. This garment is worn by a deacon over his alb and stole on special occasions.) The services of a commentator, readers, cantors, and our parish choir were arranged. Songs and readings were chosen and a program booklet was printed and assembled. Some of the men volunteered their sons as altar boys for the occasion, and two seminarians agreed to help keep things running smoothly on ordination day itself.

Since Cleveland's Cathedral of St. John the Evangelist was being remodeled, the ceremony was to take place at our parish, and some extra responsibilities fell upon Phil and me. All of the necessary facilities were reserved well in advance, and members of the Christian Family Movement volunteered to plan and to host a general reception in the school hall immediately following the ceremony. Meanwhile, Phil and I planned a family reception to follow it in our own home.

Even though all of these arrangements had been made, there was still more to be done. Each diocese is free to set its own policy on the matter, but since Bishop Hickey wanted his deacons to dress in a black suit with a Roman collar whenever they attended church functions with any of the bishops of our diocese, my husband and I went together to purchase a black suit at a local men's clothing store. Our next stop was at a Catholic religious goods store where we bought a black shirt with a white Roman collar and a long white alb in a style that looked good on my six-foot-one inch, rather-thin husband.

There remained only one garment to which I personally wanted to give some careful thought. The deacon's distinctive sign at liturgical functions is the stole which he wears over his alb. A priest wears his stole around the back of his neck, over his shoulders, and hanging long down the front on both sides. The deacon's stole is basically the same length; however, it is worn over his left shoulder. After diagonally crossing the deacon's torso, front and back, it is clasped together at the right hip and from there hangs down along his right side.

Matching stoles and dalmatics had been ordered for the men, but I wanted to do something special for Phil. Surprising him by making a stole seemed a good idea, but deciding upon something that would be just right was not easy until Phil happened to mention having seen a stole with a contemporary grapes-and-wheat design which he liked. What sign could be more fitting for one who was to serve at the Lord's table and who was being called upon to feed the multitudes through the ministries of the word, of liturgy, and of charity?

It took many hours of secret labor to design and appliqué multicolored wheat, grapes, and leaves on a white linen-like fabric. Then once the stole was finished, I neatly boxed it, wrapped the package in festive paper, and hid it in a safe place until the night before ordination.

The last of our preparations included ordering flowers for church and home and finally, two weeks before the ceremony, having banns, similar to those published before a wedding or a priestly ordination, printed in our parish bulletin and read at all of the Masses.

The rehearsal came just two days later, twelve days before the actual ceremony. To add to the excitement, the staff of our diocesan newspaper sent a photographer to take pictures for a front-page story about the diaconate and the men being ordained which was printed in the paper later that same week.

The next few days flew by. Almost before we knew it, it was the eve of ordination, but the spirit of excitement and anticipation in our home that night made it seem more like Christmas Eve. Knowing that we would be extremely busy the following day, my husband and I decided to surprise the children with a new religious record as our ordination gift to them—affirming that they, too, were an important part of the celebration. After Phil and I had all five children safely tucked into bed, we checked and rechecked our lists of things to do.

Then, Phil and I settled down on the living room sofa together. This was the moment I had been anxiously awaiting for weeks. I produced my carefully wrapped gift for Phil from its hiding place.

"Thanks, Honey, this stole is beautiful," he said, and he smiled as he proudly presented me with a silver chain from which hung a white cross enameled with blue and green flowers.

All that was left for us now was to take some time out to relax and refresh ourselves before the events of the day to come. What better way for us to relax before committing the rest of our lives to the Lord's work than by listening to some of our favorite contemporary religious records and by praying together in the soft glow of candlelight.

"Be with us, please, Lord," we prayed. "Not simply so that things will go smoothly tomorrow, but be with us all the days of our lives as we strive to serve you in the best ways we know and in the ways in which we feel you are calling us to serve. Teach us your ways, Lord, and gently lead us in this ministry to your people. Bless our marriage and our family, Lord. Bless us all. And help us to continue to grow together in this commitment to service for you. Thank you, Lord, thank you. Amen! Alleluia! Amen!"

And now we had only to wait for the beginning of a new day, a day which would begin a whole new era in our lives.

4

Ordination

Ordination day dawned bright and beautiful. Arriving early at the parish, Phil and I checked to make sure everything was in order for the ordination Mass.

After leaving the serenity of our church peacefully awaiting the drama about to unfold within its walls, we walked over to the school hall where there was utter confusion. Here, the priests, deacons, and candidates were vesting and the other men in the formation program were assembling. That group alone would have created enough confusion; however, the families of the men being ordained were gathered there, too. (Although the wives and children of the men being ordained processed on that day, in our diocese they now simply take their places in the assigned pews ahead of time.) There were so many people to greet and so many concerns being expressed that I could barely hear myself think above the noise of the crowd.

Before long, the procession was ready to leave the hall. The altar boys were in the lead with our oldest son Philip proudly carrying a candle. They were followed by the Knights of Columbus and then by the men who were in the diaconate formation program. Phil, our children, and I came next amid the families of the other men who were about to be ordained. What an excited group we were! Two Protestant ministers, more than fifty priests, and seven ordained deacons followed us. As we walked down the sidewalk toward the main entrance of Holy Family Church, we were joined by additional priests and Bishop Hickey who had vested in the rectory.

Almost before I realized it, we were at the entrance of the church. Although it seemed more like a dream, here we actually were at last, literally moving toward the moment when Phil would proclaim before our bishop, our family, and our friends his permanent, lifetime commitment to ministry as an ordained deacon for the diocese of Cleveland. It was no wonder we were both nervous; I, too, was processing toward the moment when I would be called upon to state my willingness to support Phil in his ministry for the rest of my life.

The men being ordained and their families had been assigned pews alphabetically. Ours was the front pew on the right-hand side. Phil's parents and mine were already seated when we joined them, but I still felt as if I were dreaming.

The sound of Bishop Hickey's words beginning the celebration of the Mass brought me back to reality.

Then, almost before I knew it, the greeting and the penitential rite had been completed, the "Gloria" had been sung by the choir, and the bishop had read the opening prayer.

It was time for the First Reading:

The word of the LORD came to me thus:
Before I formed you in the womb I knew you,
    before you were born I dedicated you,
    a prophet to the nations I appointed you.
"Ah, Lord GOD!" I said,
    "I know not how to speak; I am too young."
But the LORD answered me,
Say not, "I am too young."
    To whomever I send you, you shall go;
    whatever I command you, you shall speak.
Have no fear before them,
    because I am with you to deliver you, says the LORD (Jer 1:4-8).

"Yes," I thought to myself, "before these men were formed in their mothers' wombs, the Lord knew them." Before they were born, they, like the prophet Jeremiah, had been dedicated to the Lord for this ministry. Now Phil and his classmates were being appointed modern-day "prophets" for the people of our diocese.

Jeremiah's words certainly sounded much like those of my husband: "I know not how to speak; I am too young" (1:6). How symbolic of the doubts and fears Phil and I had had throughout his time in formation. From now on God would listen to no excuses. Phil and his classmates were being ordained to go forth to speak with confidence, without fear, and with the assurance that the Lord would truly be with them.

The Mass was moving rapidly along. Soon we heard the Second Reading (1 Pet 4:7-11), which ended:

> As generous distributors of God's manifold grace, put your gifts at the service of one another, each in the measure he has received. The one who speaks is to deliver God's message. The one who serves is to do it with the strength provided by God. Thus, in all of you God is to be glorified through Jesus Christ: to him be glory and dominion throughout the ages. Amen.

This reading, too, had much to say to the men, but it also had much to say to me as a wife. I knew, for the most part, it would be Phil's delivery of God's message and the sharing of his gifts, his prayer, and his love which would be visible to the world. It would have to be that way because, for the time being at least, my involvement in his diaconal ministry would be minimal. But I also knew that I too was bringing a special gift to the Church. My love, my prayers, and all that I would do for my husband and children in order to keep things running smoothly at home would be my gift to Phil's ministry. An intangible, invisible gift, but a gift nonetheless. We both knew all that we did, separately and together, would be done to bring glory to God.

The sound of the voice of one of the deacons previously ordained reading the gospel (Luke 9:18-24) brought me back to reality.

Once again, the reading which the men had chosen was filled with meaning for them. Luke 9:20, "But you—who do you say that I am?" had been the topic of lively discussion in their Scripture class. Here it seemed to be read as a sign of their total, undeniable commitment to the Lord.

It was now time for each of the six candidates for ordination to be called forward by name. Here too, a deacon previously ordained took part in the ceremony when he called each candidate in turn. Before I knew it, I was hearing, "Philip J. Mraz, Holy Family Church, Parma."

"I am ready and willing," Phil replied as he stood in the aisle alongside of our pew before returning to his place at my side.

Next, Fr. Bob Pfeiffer, in his role as diocesan director of the diaconate program, came forward and spoke: "Most Reverend Father, holy mother Church requests you to ordain our brothers here present for the office of deacon."

"Do you know if they are worthy?" the bishop queried.

"I testify that upon inquiry among the people of God, and upon recommendation of those who are specially qualified, they have been found worthy."

"My brothers," the bishop addressed the candidates, "you have committed yourselves in love to your wives and to your families. You must continue to love and to serve them as husbands and fathers strengthened in the sacrament of Holy Matrimony. Your service of the wider Christian community must be with their knowledge and their consent. Hence, we address ourselves now to your wives and to your families."

The time had come for the wives and the children of the candidates for ordination to be introduced. As a sign of our willingness to be a part of the total commitment the men were making, we stood as our names were called, and then the six wives approached the bishop.

"We are grateful to God for the example of Christian family life to which you have given witness. Throughout the formation period of your husbands, you have come to understand better the sacrifice in time and the new dimension that diaconal ministry will bring into your family and into your marriage.

"Without your support, he [your husband] could not have come to this moment, and the acceptance of ordination must be a choice shared in and accepted by you. And so, in the presence of God and the Church, I ask you, do you willingly and freely consent to the ordination of your husband?"

"I do," the six of us replied in unison.

At that moment, it had seemed right and good for me to stand before God and God's people and to promise to support Phil in his ministry. But I wondered as I returned to my place in the pew, if I had, in the past three and one-half years in formation, really come to understand the sacrifice in time and the new dimension which diaconal ministry would bring into our lives as the bishop had suggested? Once Phil was ordained, we, as a couple and a family, would no longer be a part of the tightly structured educational program which had been the basis of our preparation. Ordination was, in a way, very much like a graduation from formation. Therefore, although I knew Phil had made an informal commitment to continue his education, I was fairly certain that ordained ministry would make life after ordination different for us.

The bishop again addressed the wives. "It is our prayer that God will reward your generosity and, through the ministry of your husbands, your marriages and families may grow deeper and stronger. May the Lord help you all to persevere in this commitment."

Persevere? Was living with ordained ministry going to be more difficult than any of us realized?

At the bishop's next words stating that the six men had been chosen for the order of deacon, the church resounded with applause.

The homily and instruction followed. After explaining the role of deacons in the Church and reminding all present of the importance of their support for the men about to be ordained, Bishop Hickey cautioned the candidates that their service to the Church would be effective only to the extent that their personal commitment to Jesus remained vital and strong. I knew the bishop was right. By themselves, the men could accomplish nothing worthwhile in ministry, but through the power of Jesus promised to them through the sacrament of holy orders, they would be worthy and effective deacons. I would pray for that.

Prayer! The strength for ministry would come not only from the grace of the sacrament of holy orders but also from the deacon's prayerful union with the Lord. How important my husband's prayer life would be—mine too. In order to be the source of prayer support for Phil that I hoped to be, I would need to continue to build my own relationship with the Lord.

"It is as men of the Church that you are to serve. . . ." the bishop continued. "You shall be ordained not to do your own thing or not to do simply what may come to you at the spur of the moment. You are not to speak or to serve simply in your own name but as deacons of the Church—men who have been authorized, ordained, to serve in faithful obedience, in clear orthodoxy of teaching, and in full and complete union with your bishop and with our Holy Father, the bishop of Rome."

The most surprising remark in the homily was one which I could not even begin to comprehend at the time. The men were cautioned that their ministries of service would be accompanied by suffering. ". . . But likewise, be convinced that your sufferings will be fruitful, that you serve most effectively when you join your suffering with the Lord Jesus—when you serve together with your brother deacons and priests and your bishop."

What a strange thing for the bishop to say. It was true that our time in formation had included some "suffering," for life had sometimes been overly busy and pressured for us. However, what I found it impossible to believe now was that the overwhelming joy of this ordination ceremony could possibly be leading us to future sufferings of any kind. Surely, the bishop was mistaken.

"My brothers, be always men of deep faith, of constant hope, of burning love—deacons of the Church of Cleveland. And then, when you meet the Lord on the last day, you shall hear from him those blessed words, 'Well done my good and faithful servant. Enter into the joy of your Lord,'" Bishop Hickey concluded.

Now, it was time for the men about to be ordained to proclaim in the sight of God and in the sight of all present their intention to receive the sacrament of holy orders and their willingness to serve as deacons of the Church.

Phil and his classmates went to stand in a row before the bishop. "Are you willing to be ordained for the Church's ministry by the laying on of hands and the gift of the Holy Spirit?" he asked them.

"I am," they replied in unison.

"Are you resolved to discharge the office of deacon with humility and love in order to assist the priests to help the people of Christ?"

"I am," the candidates replied again.

"Are you resolved to hold with a clear conscience to the mystery of faith, as the apostle calls it, and to proclaim this faith in word and action taught by the gospel and the Church's tradition?"

"I am."

"Are you resolved to maintain and enrich a spirit of prayer appropriate to your way of life and, according to your situation, to fulfill faithfully the liturgy of the hours for the Church and for the whole world?" the bishop continued.

"I am."

"Are you resolved from now on to shape your way of life according to the example of Christ whose body and blood you minister at the altar?"

"I am, with the help of God," the men replied.

The questions which had been asked were in effect very much like the questions Phil had answered "I do" to on our wedding day. No wonder the ordination ceremony itself reminded me so much of a wedding. It *was* one! Phil was marrying our Church. And somehow, in a way that was yet unclear, I was to be a part of that marriage.

The time had now come for each of the men to go individually before the bishop and answer yet another question. Phil was first.

"Do you promise me and my successors obedience and respect?"

"I do," my husband replied—just as he had promised to love, honor, and cherish me on our wedding day.

"May God who began the good work in you bring it to fulfillment," Bishop Hickey told each man in turn.

We had now come to the part of the ceremony when Phil and his classmates prostrated themselves before the altar for the invitation to prayer and the Litany of the Saints. At that moment, it seemed right that my spouse should be lying on the floor offering his life to the Lord.

At long last, after the bishop's prayer concluding the litany, the actual moment of ordination was at hand. Each of the six men in turn approached the bishop and knelt prayerfully before him. Bishop Hickey, saying nothing, then laid his hands upon the candidate's head for a few seconds.

The children and I watched with a special pride and joy as the bishop, invoking the Holy Spirit, imposed hands upon Phil. By that seemingly simple act, he was now an ordained deacon and we were a deacon's family. In just a few seconds' time, what we had all worked toward and had looked forward to for so long had become a reality. Moreover, with the moment of ordination, not just Phil but our whole family was beginning the new adventure of living out that reality.

The bishop's prayer consecrating the men to a life of service followed, ending with:

Let them excel in every virtue: in sincere love, in the use of authority with moderation, in concern for the sick and the poor, in purity
and irreproachable conduct, and in a deeply spiritual life. Let your
commandments be evident in their conduct, so that the faithful
may follow their good example. Let them offer the world the witness of a clear conscience. Help them to persevere, firm and steadfast in Christ. Just as your own Son came not to be served but to
give himself in service to others, may these deacons imitate him
on earth and reign with him in heaven.

This was indeed how a deacon should try to live his life,
patterned after the life of Christ himself. But, somehow, I
knew it would not be an easy way to live.

The time had now come for the newly ordained deacons
to vest in their stoles and dalmatics. It was good that Deacon Charlie Johnson was helping me to vest Phil, for my
mind went blank. Which went on first—the stole or the
dalmatic? "The stole," Charlie told me with confidence. "It
rests on the left shoulder, crossing over to the right hip,"
he reminded me before he took over the task of helping Phil
to get the stole on properly. The dalmatic presented no
problem—once the three of us had figured out which of the
three large openings was to go over Phil's head, my husband's arms slipped through the armholes with ease.

The other couples must have been nervous, too. Out of
the corner of my eye, I saw that one of the men and his
"assistants" had put his dalmatic on backwards and the
stole was falling on the floor. That threesome was busy
removing both garments and starting all over again.

As my hands nervously smoothed the fabric of Phil's
dalmatic, I realized how proud I was of him and how proud
I was to be there alongside of him, helping him. But then,
was that not where I had been for the twelve years of our
marriage? And had I not been there for Phil in a new and
different way throughout formation—at his side, helping
and encouraging him? Standing at my husband's side now
seemed a fitting conclusion to our diaconal preparation. At
the same time, I sensed that this moment was also an indication of the beginning of a new dimension in our lives—a

dimension which would include a fuller, deeper helping on my part.

As the men vested, the church was filled with the sound of the choir singing. The words of the refrain of the song "I call you from your brothers, I send you in my name" reminded us that it was God who was sending his new deacons out into the world in his name. However, in helping Phil to vest, I had symbolically sanctioned his being sent. I was sending my husband out into the world, too—giving him freely and totally, or so I thought at the time, to the Lord to minister to his people.

It was now time to watch as the newly ordained deacons knelt in turn before Bishop Hickey who presented each with a new lectionary.

"Receive the Gospel of Christ, whose herald you are. Believe what you read, teach what you believe, and practice what you teach," the bishop instructed each of the men.

The ordination ceremony then concluded with a sign of peace and fraternity exchanged between the bishop and all the deacons. Afterwards, the newly ordained deacons took their places at the altar for the rest of the Eucharistic liturgy. Here the familiar form of the Mass resumed. The remainder of the Mass flew by. Almost before I knew it, it was time for us to leave.

I watched from my place as Deacon Phil Mraz processed out with the rest of the deacons, the bishop, and the priests; however, as I watched my husband pass our pew, I was filled with a strange combination of pride and joy mixed with a sense of loss. As Phil's wife, I was naturally proud of his accomplishments. But just a few minutes before, I had agreed to send my husband forth, and here we were separated already. In all likelihood, from here on, Phil would seldom be with me in church. It appeared that by allowing my spouse to pursue the diaconate and ordination, I had somehow given up a part of my claim to him, but then, maybe I was wrong.

Happily, in spite of the strange feeling of loss, I now had

an ordained deacon on my hands. My first challenge as the deacon's wife was to find my husband! Outside, on the sidewalk in front of the church, Phil and his classmates were so completely surrounded by well-wishers that it was almost impossible for me to get near them.

On our way to the reception, Phil and I were stopped by a photographer who posed the two of us for a picture. My husband held his lectionary in his right hand while his left was around my waist holding me close to him. That picture, taken on one of the most important days of our lives, shows Phil symbolically holding the two things most important to him—his faith, indicated by the lectionary, and our family, depicted by me.

Actually, it looked as though it might be quite some time before the children and I had Phil to ourselves again because when we reached the reception hall, many of our friends were crowded around him while numerous others were waiting to talk with him. There could be no doubt that my husband was a center of attention. Standing apart from his admirers, I realized that I felt left out. No one, it seemed, appreciated me or was even aware of my essential role in Phil's diaconate endeavor. However, I knew that without my support he would not have arrived at this moment. Moreover, without my continued support, he would not be able to continue in ministry. Could the others not see that we were a team and that this was my day, too? Apparently not. It was late that night before I was finally able to have Phil to myself again. As we sat alone on the sofa, just as we had the night before, my husband put his arm around me, and I snuggled cozily against him.

"Thank you, Lord, for today. Thank you for the gift of ordination, and thank you for all that it will bring into our lives," we prayed.

Yet, I could not help but wonder just what sort of challenges and changes ordination would bring for us. In the morning, we would begin to find out.

5

Beginning New Life in the Church

Monday, the day after ordination, Phil stayed home from work. After a leisurely breakfast, our family settled down to the next important business of the day—opening cards and gifts. In spite of the fact that the only ordination gift we had wanted was the gift of our guests' presence, many had chosen to share more as a sign of their support of Phil's diaconal ministry. There was a stack of envelopes and packages waiting to be opened, and there were five pairs of eager young hands that could hardly wait to begin exploring the contents of the gift-wrapped boxes.

This looked like it was to be similar to the day when Phil and I had opened our wedding gifts, with one big difference. At the time of our wedding, the selection of gifts had probably been stacked in my favor—sets of soft pastel towels and fancy glassware.

Now it was Phil's turn. Except for a beautiful engraved silver serving tray which was addressed to both of us, everything else was for him. There were stoles in various liturgical colors, an alb, a good pen and pencil set, books, and records—all of which were to be used in Phil's ministry. Even the greeting cards were all addressed to my husband alone.

On the day before, at the reception following ordination, I had begun to suspect that few people knew or understood how much a part of Phil's diaconal formation I had been. Now, as I watched my husband and our children opening his packages and his envelopes, I was convinced of it. It was not that I begrudged my spouse the gifts. I certainly had no use for an alb or a stole. Because we had always shared everything we had without reservation, I knew I could read Phil's books, listen to his records, or use his pens and pencils anytime I wanted.

"So what are you disturbed about?" I asked myself, and once again, I discovered I was feeling left out. To make matters worse, I was ashamed of the emotions which were welling up inside of me. My feeling a little jealous did not make any sense at all. I had known from the first that Phil was the one who would be ordained, not I. So why was I upset? Did I want recognition for my support given freely and lovingly? Whom was I doing all of this for anyway—for God, for Phil, or for myself?

"Don't be jealous," I scolded myself. I could not help but smile as I realized there was at least one good thing about all of this—I would not have to write any thank-you notes.

Thus began our first day of living with the diaconate. As Phil and I continued the process of adjusting to living out our diaconal commitment, it became more and more apparent that we had indeed "married" our Church. Moreover, in living out the promises we had made at ordination, we soon discovered that the adjustments we needed to make in our marriage to the Church closely resembled those we had once made as newlyweds.

While dating and engaged, Phil and I had come to know each other fairly well. However, it was only after the exchange of our wedding vows that we had gone home to our cozy apartment. It was only then that we came to really know what living together as husband and wife would mean for us.

The new Mr. and Mrs. Philip J. Mraz embarked upon married life with a honeymoon that lasted for months. We were so much in love, and our life together was all I could have dared to hope it would be. But gradually, we discovered that neither of us was the ideal person each had thought the other to be and marriage was not always the fairy-tale experience the world had once led us to believe it would be. As our growing list of disadvantages to living our married life lengthened, the constant, cozy, loving relationship which I had assumed would last forever, decreased and eventually almost disappeared. Phil and I were both disillusioned with marriage. The novelty and exitement of new love was gone; all the days seemed to be the same. It was then that a tension began to build between us, and deep, meaningful communication became rare. Both my husband and I felt isolated, alone, and miserable. Eventually, there was doubt in my mind about whether or not married life was good for us.

Not being particularly fond of wasting time being miserable, we rather quickly began asking ourselves some pertinent questions. "Are we still in love?" "Would we be better off divorced?" These questions and others, prompted by our brief, but necessary, periods of disillusionment and misery,* were hard to face and hard to answer, but out of the answers came a whole new way of life for us.

Phil and I did love each other. In addition, we had made a commitment to a lifetime together. Therefore, as husband and wife, we made the definite, conscious decision to make our marriage better. Eventually, a return to deep, meaningful communication* as well as more frequent working and playing together brought us to a new closeness beyond any we had experienced before. The hardships were still present, of course, but the burdens when shouldered by two were much lighter than when we had been trying to carry

*For a discussion of related ideas in the broader context of marriage, *see* Urban G. Steinmetz, *Marriage Enrichment Program*, Recorded Lecture Series (Escanaba, Mich.: Family Enrichment Bureau, 1965) session 1.

them alone. Even the smallest joys found in our day to day living were greater when shared in love. At last, we had arrived at the point where we were contented with married life, and it was comfortable, right, and good for us.

Phil and I had been living contentedly for several years when the courtship-engagement-marriage cycle began all over again. This time, however, we were the groom and the Church was the bride. We had been courting the idea of adding the diaconate to our lives before applying for admission to the program. Then, during the formation years, our diaconate engagement period, we had had continuous opportunities to become more and more familiar with the diaconate and our Church. Finally, together, we had approached ordination—the ceremony in which Phil, and I too, had promised to love, honor, and obey the commands of our faith. Separately, we had answered our "I do's." We had become ordained husband and supportive wife wedded to our Church in a union that would last a lifetime.

However, it was only after returning to our cozy ranch home to live with this new dimension in our lives that we began to really know what living together as Deacon and Mrs. Philip J. Mraz would mean.

As busy as the first few months following ordination were for us, they were definitely our diaconate honeymoon. Phil and I were in love with each other and in love with the diaconate. Wearing his new alb and the grapes-and-wheat stole I had made, Phil had assisted our pastor at a Mass of Thanksgiving celebrating his diaconal ordination. My deacon husband had a sense of good liturgy, functioned well at the altar, and seemed to be at ease there. Our parish priests encouraged Phil, and under our pastor's watchful eye, the parish's newest staff member was being allowed the freedom to function as fully as he wished. In spite of the fact that our parish had never had a permanent deacon before, Phil's ministry at the altar and in parish programs seemed to be accepted by the majority of the parishioners. Just as importantly, our Christian Family Movement friends were obviously proud to have a diocesan deacon involved in their activities.

Support and affirmation for our new deacon abounded at home, too. Our children had no complaints, and neither did I. Watching my husband minister to God's people, the words of the first reading at ordination would come back to me: "Before I formed you in the womb, I knew you, before you were born I dedicated you, a prophet to the nations I appointed you" (Jer 1:5). I was proud of my deacon and his accomplishments knowing in my heart that Phil had been created for ordained ministry. Moreover, amid the busyness of our new committed life-style, I soon discovered that my feelings of being left out and unappreciated had disappeared. Just as I had been happy to be in Phil's arms as his bride, I was now happy to see him in the arms of his Church through his ordination. And I, too, was happy to be in the arms of our Church through my limited sharing in my husband's ministry.

"I'm so proud of you!" "Sure, it's fine with me if you're gone another night this week." These and other words of love and affirmation commonly emanated from my mouth.

So went our diaconate honeymoon. I can not recall how long it actually lasted; however, with the passage of time, things began to change. Slowly but surely, my deacon husband and I began to discover some disillusioning disadvantages to living out our diaconal commitment. At first, I viewed the drawbacks as only minor inconveniences that would eventually disappear on their own. Unfortunately, as my list of inconveniences continued to grow, not one item on the list disappeared. It was then that a comment made earlier by the wife of another newly ordained deacon began to make sense. "Now that the excitement is over," she had told me, "I feel a little bit lost, maybe let down. Or maybe I'm depressed."

Although, at the time, I had been puzzled by her remark, I was now beginning to experience the same feelings. Living the diaconate was becoming less and less the fairy-tale experience I had once envisioned. Of course, I was not completely naive; before ordination I had suspected that living with the diaconate would not always be easy. But now I was finding endless evidence to support my suspicions.

It took no detective with a magnifying glass to discover that the first and most obvious problem was scheduling. As increasing ministerial demands were placed upon Phil, our lives became busier and more complicated. Life had been so much easier when we had simply been required to show up for diaconate events which someone else had scheduled. However, with ordination, we had been separated from the structured formation program upon which we had come to rely so heavily. We had been thrust out into the real world and left to our own devices. Without our realizing it at the time, Phil and I had experienced culture shock, and now that we were completely in charge of our lives once again, things were getting out of hand. There did not seem to be anything we could do about it because everything we had committed ourselves to with our family, Phil's work, and ministry seemed important.

When newly ordained, Phil had been careful not to become overly involved in ministry. However, as time passed, there were more and more requests for his presence outside of our home. In spite of our pastor's wise warning not to take on too much, my new deacon was finding it harder and harder to answer no to some of the requests being made of him. How could Phil refuse when everywhere he looked there was such a need for ministry? And how could I possibly blame him for saying yes so many times? I saw the same needs he saw. I knew he had been ordained to minister to those needs; therefore, I certainly did not want to be the one to hold him back. At the same time, I was torn, for I was not entirely happy with the way my husband's ministry was taking him away from home so much. However, Phil was not entirely to blame, for both of us had been answering too many yeses where there should have been a few nos.

Unfortunately, parish, diocesan, and C.F.M. events as well as the monthly diaconate meetings and occasional retreats and ceremonies seemed to be falling wherever they had a mind to on our busy schedule. Of course, it was not only the diaconate that was complicating our lives. The children had a variety of activities of their own, and, among other things, I was facilitating a new parenting program initiated in our area. Never sure what was on the schedule, I was constantly checking the calendar to see what was happening next. Since neither Phil nor I always remembered to list our activities, that did not necessarily provide me with the information I was seeking.

"I have a meeting this evening, Honey," my husband remarked casually at supper.

"You can't! There's nothing on the calendar!" I exclaimed. "All day I've been counting on going alone to the shopping mall tonight."

"I guess I forgot to mark the calendar," Phil remarked nonchalantly.

Although my disappointment was obvious, my feelings did not seem to bother my deacon in the way I thought they should. My retort was swift in coming. "Well, I guess you forgot to write it down! And I guess you forgot to tell me, too!"

Actually, my spouse may have mentioned the meeting to me; however, if he did, I had forgotten. Phil had been claiming to have told me things frequently, but I certainly was not remembering his having mentioned them. Perhaps he had told me, and I had forgotten. Or perhaps our problem was that I was sometimes too busy to take the time to concentrate on what my husband was saying. If either was the case, I was not about to admit it to my spouse. Come to think of it, I had been a little lax about writing down my occasional activities, too, but I was not about to admit that either.

"Maybe things will work out better for us if the first one

to write something on the calendar for the day gets first choice," Phil suggested.

"Maybe so," I murmured as I fought the almost irresistible urge to grab the calendar and quickly mark *"DOTTIE— SHOPPING"* in big bold letters in the square for the day. Phil's new plan for scheduling was certainly worth a try. But since my husband's activities were usually scheduled in advance and mine were most often last-minute decisions, I knew I was the one most likely to lose out in this new arrangement.

Our over-scheduling and forgetting to mark things on the calendar were further complicated by the fact that things seemed to happen in clumps. And more and more often there was less and less time that elapsed between clumps of activities. During the weeks when Phil was especially busy, he was often gone more than one or two nights. This did not even include time for Phil to honor the informal commitment he had made to continue his religious education. Trying to find time for another diaconate event on our schedule was out of the question.

How could this have happened when not so long before, at our final interview with the diaconate staff, I had stated so positively that Phil's being gone two evenings a week was all I felt would be acceptable to me and good for our family? It was no wonder I had hidden our overly full family calendar where no visitor would be able to see it. Horizontally, vertically, diagonally, no matter which direction I looked, there always seemed to be a diaconate bingo in the squares for each month. Unfortunately, Deacon Phil and his wife Dottie were not winning at this game.

The diaconate seemed to assume that it had a right to first place in our lives. Phil had always taken pride in his work as an electrician; it was a top priority, too. It had to be—after all, that was the way my spouse was providing for the needs of our growing family. Somehow our family had ended up in last place on our list of priorities.

The detective in me had discovered the culprits, or so

I thought. Time had definitely become our enemy, and that all important ministry was taking so much time that it was pushing other activities which had once been important to us out of our lives. "Yes, there are two felons in this case," I decided. "Ministry is the thief stealing our time."

Our lives had become pressured, and unfortunately, rather than drawing us closer together, the tensions were driving us apart. Time to nurture our relationship was hard to come by. Where Phil and I had once played, there was now little, if any, time for play. Where we had once worked together on projects at home and at church, there was now little time for such things. My deacon husband and I had begun living out our ordination commitment by praying together; now we were not praying together at all. As a couple committed to ministry to others, we had ceased ministering to our own and to each other's spirits.

Furthermore, Phil's ordination had once been a goal which we had worked toward together. Now that it had been attained, Phil seemed to be completely on his own in ministry while I was left behind to see to things at home. Where there had once been a definite "wifely" feeling within me, I now occasionally felt like the live-in maid, and that certainly was not doing anything to enhance our husband-wife relationship.

I could not bring myself to talk to Phil about what I was thinking and feeling. Loving him, I did not want to hurt him, nor did I want to burden my busy husband with my problems, pains, fears, or frustrations. Although I had been in the habit of telling Phil everything, I was now sharing very little. So was he. When we did take the time to talk, we were often so preoccupied with our own thoughts that we seldom heard what the other was saying. Once again, deep, meaningful communication between us had virtually ceased.

I soon discovered that we were not alone in our problems; the comments of other deacons' wives proved that.

"Even when my husband's home, he's not home," one wife told me. "His mind is on ministry—planning a program or preparing a homily—whatever is next on his schedule. He spends so much time in a quiet corner by himself that the children and I hardly know he is there."

"On Sundays, I'm a liturgical widow. During the week, I'm a ministry widow," another wife shared.

If she was referring to feeling alone and empty, there were others of us who knew only too well what this woman was talking about. None of us had consented to be a part of our husbands' commitments only to feel like widows. Diaconate or not, we were all too young for that.

"Better at church than in a bar," another woman consoled herself. But was it better? I was beginning to wonder whether it made any difference where Phil went when he was not at home.

All clues pointed to the fact that our marriage was definitely suffering. In spite of the fact that except for diaconate meetings and special events my remaining behind had more or less become a way of life for us during formation, living with ordained ministry was different. Too often Phil seemed to have much less time, attention, and affection for his first spouse, me, than he had for his second spouse, the Church. It was as if I were losing my husband to another woman, but what was I to do when the other woman in Phil's life was holy mother Church? As Phil's spouse by his first marriage, I was becoming increasingly resentful of the time he spent with his new bride while I was left in almost total charge of things at home.

But time, ministry, and the change in our marriage relationship were not the only things causing me problems. I must have been a super sleuth to ferret out negative feelings, for I certainly was able to come up with a lengthy list of them. As my list of disillusionments grew, my idealistic view of living the diaconate as a cozy addition to our lifestyle gradually disappeared. The novelty and excitement of our commitment was gone; the sacrifices and the sufferings were uppermost in my mind. It was no wonder I was not a very happy person, often tense and irritable.

"Why can't things work out smoothly without much effort on our part?" I wondered. "After all, Phil is an ordained clergyman." However, the word "ordained" did not seem to make any impression upon the life-style into which we had fallen, and the tension which had built up within me left me feeling much like a volcano ready to explode. Although I was surprised by the inevitable eruption when it finally occurred, I suppose I really should not have been.

One evening my handsome deacon husband, dressed in his black clergy suit complete with white Roman collar and ready to leave to do something that was in my mind important, leaned over to give me a kiss as I stood knee deep in laundry. There was no end in sight to Phil's being gone—or to the dirty clothes for that matter. I was miserable. I knew I would be spending another night supporting my deacon by babysitting and catching up on work around the house. I did not want Phil's kiss. All I wanted was for him to leave me alone.

"When the children are grown," I snapped, "you might as well move into the rectory! The kids need you now, but once they are gone, why should I keep house for someone I never see?"

Phil was crushed, and I could not believe I had made that hurtful remark. It was really out of character for me to treat my spouse that way; however, at that particular moment, the feelings were real.

"Jealousy, resentment, frustration, anger, self-pity— what kinds of feelings are these for the wife of an ordained clergyman to have?" I scolded myself.

"Very real ones," was the obvious reply. But at the same time, I was feeling guilty about the feelings I was experiencing.

The word "divorce" even managed to make its way into my head that night. "A divorced deacon ministering to marriage and family—now I wonder what the Church would think about that?'' I thought as I raised my eyebrows. ''Especially if the divorce came *after* ordination because the deacon was no longer satisfactorily fulfilling his role as husband and father.''

That evening, for the first, and I think the only, time, I was ready to tell Phil, ''Forget it! Let's turn in your alb and stole and be normal, everyday people again with a normal, everyday marriage and family life.'' Enough was enough and I had had it.

As terrible as I felt about erupting with such vehemence, the explosion was the best thing that could possibly have happened. The heat of the moment had not only brought forth a violent outpouring of the feelings I had been keeping from Phil, but it had also caused a flow of questions all of which seemed to need answers.

What was happening to our lives? Ministry had become a duty—all of the fun had gone out of it. It seemed I was no longer in love with ordained service to the people of God; was I even in love with the deacon who went with that ministry? If so, then why was I the least help to Phil when he was the busiest and needed my help the most? Maybe I was not cut out to be a deacon's wife after all. Or perhaps this was all there was for us—an overfilled calendar with a husband and father not present as often as his wife and family would like. Maybe our marriage and family would be better off if we divorced the diaconate program and ministry altogether.

''How could a loving Father have called us to this?'' I wondered. In fact, had God even called us to the diaconate in the first place? Had Phil's ordination been a mistake? ''I thought we were following your lead, Lord. If that is true, why are our lives so messed up? Where are you in all of this anyway? Are you even there?''

Not wanting our problems to continue to build and not expecting them to disappear on their own, Phil and I knew it was time for us to sit down and talk.

''Okay,'' he said as we both collapsed in our living room

after a busy day. "What's been happening to us? I used to feel that the two of us were a diaconate team. Lately I've felt as though I've become a team of one. No matter how much others seem to need me or appreciate my efforts, if ministry is the cause of the tension that has built up between us, then any good I have done will have been for nothing. Maybe I should just turn in my alb and stole and call it quits."

"Oh, no!" I gasped. "I was thinking the same thing last night when I exploded, but I have done a lot of soul-searching since then."

By opening up and taking time to talk, Phil and I were able to share the thoughts we had been keeping inside—surprisingly similar thoughts. Simply expressing what we were feeling helped both of us, and knowing that each was understanding and accepting of the honest feelings of the other helped even more.

From our discussion, it was obvious that we were both unhappy with the way our lives had been going. But we could not lay the blame on my two former suspects, time and ministry, nor could we accuse God, the diaconate program, our pastor, parish, or C.F.M. friends. I had finally solved the case. There were two culprits all right! Phil and I were the ones responsible for allowing disillusionment and misery to enter our lives. The fault was ours alone. No arrest or prosecution was necessary. We had already paid the price and were ready to reform.

Now it was time for action. We were two more or less mature adults who were ultimately responsible for our own actions, and the time had come for us to begin accepting that responsibility. If living the diaconate was going to work for us, Phil and I were the ones who would have to make it work. No one else could do that. The choice was ours—to go on being miserable, to ask to be relieved of our diaconal ministry, or to make some definite, positive changes in our attitudes and our actions in order to turn our lives around. For Phil and for me, there could be only one choice.

6

Putting Our Lives in Order

Loving each other, Phil and I had committed ourselves to a lifetime of marriage. Deep within, we knew that our call and our commitment to the diaconate were just as valid. So as husband and wife, together, we made the conscious decision to make living the diaconate good for us as individuals and for our marriage. In order to do that, the many disillusioning diaconate discoveries we had made needed to be faced head-on, accepted, evaluated, and any necessary changes in our life-style made. Here again, just as it had been when we were newlyweds, deep, meaningful communication had been the first step in improving our lives. By openly discussing all that had been bottled up inside of us, Phil and I had been freed to start over, freed to change, and freed to grow.

Once we began talking and listening to each other, ordering our priorities was the next step in turning our lives around. "Family first, then work, and finally the diaconate" had been preached so often during formation, but somehow in the busyness of our new life-style we had forgotten what was most important.

There was no doubt about it. Our family had to come first, and family had to begin with our marriage relationship. Long before we had been called to the diaconate, Phil and I had been called to be there for each other. As Phil's wife, I needed him to be my husband, lover, companion, and best friend all rolled into one. And I needed to become Phil's wife, lover, companion, and best friend once again.

The little surprises my husband planned for me helped to provide romance for the wife and lover in me. But I could not leave all of the romance-making to Phil; my husband and lover needed to know I cared, too.

As companions, working toward goals had always been good for us and for our marriage, but it now seemed that ordained ministry was like the proverbial golden ring which people reached for on an old-fashioned merry-go-round. Once you were fortunate enough to get hold of the golden ring and have it safely grasped in your hand, whatever were you supposed to do with it? The challenge and fun of reaching for the ring would suddenly disappear, and, I would think, the pleasure of holding it would most likely have created a void where the challenge had once been.

So, too, with diaconate. During formation, diaconal ordination was something Phil and I had spent three and a half years reaching for, working toward, and planning for, together. We had never quite grasped it, of course, until his ordination. Then there had been the immediate pleasure of possessing the diaconate for the first few months, followed by a void. Holding the diaconal golden ring safely in our hands, we no longer had a goal we were working toward together.

If we as a married couple wished to remain companions, then it was time to formulate new goals for ourselves. Whether the plans we were making were for a family vacation, home improvements, or something that would be happening soon in Phil's ministry made no difference. We needed to be working together toward something—another golden ring waiting to be reached for, grasped, held, and enjoyed before we moved on to the next one waiting beyond.

There was also a need as best friends to spend time sharing with each other.

"Anywhere my husband is going alone, I try to go with him—*anywhere!*" one of the wives once told me. "Even if he drives to the post office at 11:30 at night, I go with him. I may be in my robe and slippers with my hair up in rollers, but I go!

"Then we'll often order something at the drive-thru window of a local fast-food place and sit in the parking lot talking and praying together. It's great, really great! I grab at the chances my husband and I have to be alone together. If we don't take advantage of those times, we'll never have time for *us*," she continued.

I, too, prized my time with Phil; and as far as I was concerned, confiding our innermost thoughts and feelings was just as important as sharing our activities. Here was where Phil and I, as spouses and best friends, found that discussing life, sharing our faith, praying, and reading Scripture together was good for us, too. Eventually, our most intimate moments as husband and wife were those when we shared our spirituality because the sharing of our faith came from the depths of our spiritual beings, an intimacy far deeper than any other.

Phil and I had learned a painful lesson. We could not look to others to order our lives for us because, ultimately, the only ones we could rely upon for help were God and each other. Realizing this, we continuously looked to the Lord for direction as we attempted to work together in all things.

When we were working as partners in accomplishing all that needed to be done, things just naturally ran more smoothly. Problems in all areas of our lives, ministry included, did not cease to exist; they did, however, seem less difficult to handle because we were sharing them and working at overcoming them together. By keeping a better watch on his diaconate events in a conscious effort not to over-schedule, my husband was able to expend a fair share of his time, his energy, his love, and his attention on me. In time, our combined efforts aimed at improving all areas of our relationship brought Phil and me to a closeness far beyond any I would ever have dreamed possible. Surprisingly, when our first commitment to loving each other was being satisfied, that love actually nourished and enhanced the other areas of our lives. I was no longer jealous of Phil's ministry or of his time away. Of course, when our priorities were in proper order, there was less time away.

As Phil's presence at home increased, family resumed its rightful place in our order of priorities. Next on our list came Phil's work as an electrician, and finally, now properly relegated to last place, came ministry. Now, rather than our family's activities being largely planned around ministerial events, our diaconate schedule was once again working around that of our family.

Although diaconal ministry often continued to make its appearance in clumps on our calendar, it was becoming more difficult to find diaconate bingos in any direction. This time, even when they existed, Deacon Phil and his wife were winning the game, for we seemed to be handling the busy times better, too. Where I had once been most difficult to live with at precisely the times when Phil was busiest, I was now making every effort to support him. We had even taken to scheduling our own reprieves from busyness—a night out, a day away. Life had slowed down a bit, and there was a new sense of freedom as Phil and I discovered we were perfectly capable of taking charge of our own lives.

Finally, at last, once and for all, I had developed a new confidence in my feeling that Phil's diaconal ministry was indeed in response to a legitimate call from God to ordained service. I would never again doubt that Phil had been born to be ordained for the service of the Church of Cleveland. Seeing my husband fulfill his destiny and knowing that I had an important part in it was a source of great pride and joy for me. How freeing that was, and what a change from the way we had been living such a short time before.

However, the changes in our attitudes and in our life-style had not come about without considerable effort on our part. Nor had they happened overnight, but rather gradually, over a period of time, as Phil and I had worked to make our marriage in the diaconate better. It was here where the perseverance the bishop had spoken of at ordination had been an essential ingredient in making our lives more manageable and in our accepting the constant challenge to keep them that way. By no means could we ever have claimed to have had our priorities in order all of the time. We had a long way to go to accomplish that, but at least we were working at it.

Our marriage to each other and our marriage to the Church were combined as one, and as one they cycled through a delightful honeymoon, to a period of disillusionment, to a time of alarming misery to culminate in our living in a state of contented commitment.

Fortunately, our time of disillusionment and misery had been short-lived, and surprisingly, as painful as these stages of our adjustment period had been, they had been good for us. The questions they had prompted had been difficult to answer. Yet, all that Phil and I had been through in order to find the answers which were right for us had caused much growth within each of us, growth which had ultimately led to an inner sense of joy combined with peaceful satisfaction. As a result of our having faced the questions and having found reasonable answers, a whole new, very special way of life had emerged for us.

Although our diaconate life-style was often far from perfect, Phil and I were able to settle down to a new and fuller way of contented married life than we had ever known before. Once again, as man and wife, we were truly present for each other. We completed each other. Our marriage in the diaconate was secure, and living with the diaconate had become comfortable, right, and good. In coming to occupy its natural, rightful place, the diaconate had indeed become so much a part of us that it was impossible to separate it from the rest of our lives. In fact, we needed it to make our lives complete, for without it, there would have been a painful void which nothing else could possibly have filled.

When I shared my thoughts on the stages of adjustment which I felt Phil and I had gone through with another deacon's wife, she posed some interesting questions: "Do you think once you have been through the honeymoon, disillusionment, and misery, you are always living contentedly with the diaconate? Or do you think you cycle through the stages time and time again?"

"*Once* is enough for anyone to go through them!" was my immediate reply.

"I think I cycle," she related. "I think I'm on my second or third time around right now. I just finished being miserable and am feeling pretty happy with the way things are again."

After reflecting on my friend's thoughts and my own experience, I decided that maybe we were both right. Once having made it to the stage of loving commitment, I was always there. But the other stages seemed to recur from time to time within that stage.

There had been times long after ordination when I had experienced feelings similar to those I had felt when Phil was newly ordained, but they were never quite like the feelings of elation which had followed ordination itself.

Then too, the second time through disillusionment was not nearly as disturbing as the first. Already familiar with the disadvantages that came along with Phil's ordination, I found they were no longer earthshaking and had few, if any, new revelations. As for living in misery, I had done that once. Once was enough. I was not about to spend any more time miserable than was absolutely necessary.

Actually there was a comfort in having previously experienced the disadvantages and misery because, having made it through the stages once, we were never again faced with the hopeless feelings we had experienced in our first time through the misery stage. We knew, too, that together we had been able to handle the difficulties in the past. Although the diaconate had to be put back into its proper place in our lives more than once, after the first time, it became a comfortable, here-we-go-again experience as we took whatever actions were necessary to move back into living contentedly with diaconal ministry.

Because of the growth and changes which had occurred within us and within our marriage as Phil and I adjusted to living with the diaconate, we were now ready to face together the numerous challenges ordained ministry had created in all areas of our lives. What better place for me to begin to face those challenges than to explore just what it meant to be a deacon's wife?

7

The Role of a Deacon's Wife

In trying to put into words what being a deacon's wife means, I came to the conclusion that we women who were married to deacons were basically the same wives we had always been. However, in saying "I do" at our husbands' ordinations, we had become their diaconate teammates and had unknowingly committed ourselves to a series of new challenges, concerns, and responsibilities.

For me, being a deacon's wife meant seeing to my husband's and family's needs in much the same fashion as I always had. Cooking, cleaning, washing, ironing, sewing, taxiing the children, and helping to maintain our house and yard were all part of my normal routine. However, following ordination, the more my husband's ministry involvement increased, the more I was left to contend with at home. Each of the roles I had always fulfilled as a homemaker had taken on new meaning.

Cooking now meant planning our family's supper hour around Phil's schedule for the evening. Cleaning included dusting the stack of books and papers for my deacon's current projects and moving assorted things that I did not know what to do with to his already overcrowded dresser. Washing occasionally included a black shirt and a long white alb, while designing and stitching stoles in various liturgical colors had been added to my hobby of sewing. Even the taxi service we had been providing for our children was different for I found myself nearly in full charge. My job in the maintenance department had changed, too. When the fuse for my dryer blew out, I replaced it before Phil came home from work. Never before had this electrician's wife considered doing such a thing. When the washing machine broke, I called a repair service, knowing full well that Phil would not have the time to repair it soon. When the car stalled in traffic, I had it fixed.

Apparently other diaconate couples were experiencing the same phenomena:

"My husband is never home when I need him to do things around the house," one wife complained. "My list of things for him to do is ever-expanding. And my work is never done."

"I resent my husband's having free time to relax when I am still working around the house," another wife related. "Yet, one of my biggest concerns is that my husband doesn't relax enough. So, I feel especially guilty when I resent his taking some time for himself."

My friends' comments raised two other important points—the need for time for things that only our husbands could do around the house and the need for time for them to relax and to refresh themselves.

In the past I had never felt a need to be overly concerned about Phil's health—physical, social, emotional, or spiritual. He had always taken reasonably good care of himself. However, with the onset of his diaconate busyness, time for my husband's personal well-being became rare.

"I don't have time right now," Phil told me when I confronted him with the fact that the word "tennis" had virtually disappeared from his calendar. "Don't worry. I get plenty of physical exercise pulling electrical wire at work, playing ball in the backyard with the children in the summer, and shoveling snow in the winter."

However, that was not the kind of exercise I had in mind. By encouraging Phil to spend time recreating with his friends, I was seeing not simply to his physical health but to his social and emotional health as well. Time with his friends, with or without me along, was essential for my husband's social well-being, and getting away from the stress and tension of home, work, and diaconate had to be good for his emotional well-being.

Then, in order to help foster Phil's spiritual health, I encouraged my spouse to take some time for quiet, personal prayer each day and to take advantage of opportunities for community prayer, including days of recollection and retreats.

I hoped that my actions as Phil's personal health counselor would help to refresh him and relieve much of the stress that the diaconate had added to his life.

In addition to my increased concern for all aspects of Phil's health, his ministry itself was placing some new and unexpected responsibilities upon me as his diaconate teammate. Making phone calls, typing letters and bulletin announcements, and being alert to all of my husband's needs and to his busy schedule placed me in the role of the deacon's private secretary.

But surprisingly, another role which I had unknowingly assumed was that of my husband's protector. Phil had been my knight in shining armor for many years, but it seemed that as the deacon's wife, I had unconsciously become the fair maiden who stood in front of my deacon with my arms outstretched trying to protect him from his foe whom I saw as *anyone* or *anything* that could hurt him in any way. I was attempting to protect Phil from the whole world—including himself.

It would have been foolish of me to think that everyone would like my husband, as likeable as he was to me, or, for that matter, that they would appreciate his ministry. But I did want to be sure that as many as possible would accept Phil and appreciate his efforts. My first major concern

as his defender was to protect my husband and his ministry from adverse comments from those to whom he was
ministering. To accomplish this I returned to my former
profession of teaching by showing by my words and actions
just what diaconal ministry was all about.

In addition, following ordination, Phil knew he could
expect to hear a whole litany of questions before he left
home for his diaconal ministry. "Do you have your alb? Is
your stole the proper liturgical color? Do you have your lectionary? Your homily notes? Everything you need?" Listening to Phil's plans for a prayer service or a program he was
working on, I became a sounding board for his ideas, and
I was constantly informed about what was happening in
his ministry.

Most often, deacons' wives become their husbands'
toughest critics, especially when it comes to listening to ideas
for homilies. "Occasionally, I find I can make some helpful
suggestions about content, and I have to admit that hearing
my ideas expressed from the pulpit from time to time is exciting," one wife shared.

For us, my serving as ministry consultant had two additional advantages. Having my spouse ask for and value
my opinion was personally gratifying to me, but it also
served to draw us ever closer in our relationship as a married couple.

With time, as I saw Phil was doing well, I began to relax
and worry less about his acceptance. "Are you sure you
have everything?" became my single query when Phil was
leaving to minister. What a change from the litany of questions my husband had faced when he was newly ordained.
Listening to his homilies from the pew, I simply trusted that
they would be good—nervously trusted maybe, but trusted
nonetheless. Despite the fact that Phil kept his homilies
short and to the point, no matter how long he had been
ordained, anytime my deacon spoke before a group, I was
nervous for him.

Although my shepherding of Phil's ministry had undoubtedly made me his toughest critic, I knew I was also his biggest fan. How proud I was when he assisted at the altar, started something new in our parish, or made some constructive changes in an existing program.

Letting Phil know just how proud I was of him and of the commitment he had made was one important part of my role as fan; being loyal to him at all times was the other. Of course, there were some others to whom it was appropriate to express my occasional discontentment with our diaconal life-style. Phil had a right, a need, to know what I was feeling, for communication was the basis of our relationship. Sharing what we were feeling deep inside with others in the diaconate community was profitable for those of us who were deacon and wife, too, for it showed us we were not alone in what we were experiencing. An occasional comment to a close friend when I was feeling depressed or overworked did not hurt either. But my complaining to members of our parish community meant my taking a chance on harming not only our marriage but also Phil's reputation and his ministry. No matter how I was feeling at the moment, I knew I needed to be a loyal fan of my spouse and of his service for the Church.

As Phil's protector, I felt a need to safeguard my husband from more than simply those to whom he ministered. With our busy life-style, my role as family focuser came in handy. Not wanting to hurt others who were close to us or to have them blame the diaconate for the scarcity of our presence, particularly Phil's, I made a valiant attempt to be aware of what was happening in the lives of others. Being alert to the needs of our family and friends—whether it involved our being present for celebrations, helping with a project, or simply being understanding listeners—was all a part of my job. "Don't forget, there's a cub scout meeting on Friday." "It's your Mom's birthday. How about our going to visit her tonight?" My busy husband frequently heard these and other reminders.

When I concentrated on the focusing, Phil and I were

able to work together in accomplishing what was important to us at any given moment. Focusing on what was most important helped to keep our priorities in order and a balance in our lives, both essential in order for our family to avoid stormy weather.

Another role a deacon's wife assumes is that of the family barometer. Somewhere along the line, I acquired an increasing sensitivity to the moods, feelings, and needs of all family members—a sensitivity which kept me in touch with the emotional climate in our home. Phil could always tell by the look on my face, coupled with the tone of my voice, just what our family's atmospheric pressure was for the day. When my face read "stormy," my spouse knew it was time to find out why so that together we could take the appropriate actions to restore fair weather to our household. In this way our family was protected from the danger of being blown apart by the extra turbulence the diaconate had added to all of our lives.

When I sensed that Phil was becoming his own worst enemy by overworking, it was time for me to protect him from himself by becoming the household foot stomper. "No, not another thing this week!" "How about slowing down and taking some time for yourself?" These and similar comments helped protect my deacon who in his enthusiasm and desire to minister had a tendency to overdo from time to time.

On the other hand, when I sensed that Phil might be hurting because he was putting himself down or feeling discouraged, I became his cheerleader standing on the sidelines. Flashing him a big smile from my place in the crowd could boost his self-confidence when he was nervous about delivering a homily or speaking to a group. "How proud I am of you!" I would tell him. It was no lie. Phil was doing well in his endeavors, and his actions were making a difference in our community—a fact that I felt free to remind him of whenever I thought it necessary.

When Phil seemed frustrated by his inability to do more

for others, I would remind him that, for the time being, raising our children would continue to take much of our time. Later, when the children were grown, we would both be freer to perform works of charity outside of our home.

One additional, very effective way of showing my support for and confidence in my husband was by becoming his prayer partner. Once we realized the importance of praying together, at least a few minutes of shared prayer became an essential part of every day. Whenever possible, I attended the annual diaconate couples' retreat with my husband. In that way, we were able to grow spiritually, together and as individuals, in a shared experience. In addition, while Phil was off ministering, by trying to spend at least a few minutes asking God to bless my spouse in his work, I became his prayer support. Eventually I came to realize that remaining at home to care for our children when often I would have liked to have been with Phil helping him in his ministry was a prayer itself.

However, having had what I considered an important part in Phil's formation, I wanted, perhaps needed, to have a more active and important part in his ministry, too. I may not have been ordained, but I certainly had no trouble recognizing ways in which I could actively share in Phil's ordained ministry. In spite of the fact that I enjoyed my family and knew the things I was doing at home were important to us all, I sometimes found myself frustrated by my limited part as diaconal team manager. I could not help but envy the deacon's wives whose children were grown. Surely, most of them were freer to help their husbands if they so chose.

Here was where Phil's encouragement was essential to keep *me* going. ''Thanks for having my things ready for the pre-baptism program when I got home from work.'' ''There were some nice comments about my homily this morning. I really appreciate the ideas you shared and your encouragement.'' ''Thanks for getting the lawn watered today. I wasn't looking forward to doing it tonight.'' These and other of my husband's comments helped to assure me that my role in our diaconate endeavor was important and appreciated. Meanwhile, I looked forward to the time when I would be able to participate more fully in Phil's diaconal ministry.

Knowing the reality of living a busy family life with a house full of growing children and having Phil value the little managerial things I was doing, helped me to accept my quiet, supportive role as a special ministry and a gift in itself to my husband, my family, my Church, and my God. How proud I was of Phil. How proud I was to be his quiet support. How proud I was as, with the passage of time, I noticed the continued quiet admiration of others for both Phil and his work.

"But have you ever been jealous of your husband?" one of the wives asked me. "I mean not only of his time away from you, but also of the admiration other women have for him?" The time away, I understood; the "other women" I had never experienced.

"I couldn't find my husband at a social get-together after a special liturgy," she continued.

"That's not unusual," I smiled, much relieved. "Phil and I have the same trouble finding each other in crowds."

But my friend was not smiling as she continued to relate her experience. "When I asked around, someone had seen my husband talking to a woman in an office down the hall. That in itself would not have been bad, but someone else had just told me that particular woman was *in love* with my husband. While I was getting my own pastry and coffee, my deacon husband was getting refreshments for this 'other woman.'

"The worst part about it was that when I told my husband what I knew and about how jealous I was when I saw for myself that he was talking, alone, with that particular woman, he couldn't understand. 'You're being silly. You're reading things into it,' he told me. But I knew I wasn't. That woman had her eyes on my husband. This was a whole new experience for me as I had never been jealous of him before, and I had a real problem handling the situation. Fortunately, the woman has moved out of the parish. However, it seems there actually are women out there running after men in collars, and I'm determined that no one will get my husband!"

I was quite certain I would never be jealous of other women in Phil's life—the ones who worked with him on projects or who expressed their admiration for him. At least that was what I thought until one evening after a prayer service. I volunteered to take Phil's things to the car, load them all in, and move the car closer to the hall where a social get-together was being held. The night was cold, and the briefcase, record player, and records were heavy and awkward to carry.."The servant's servant" I reminded myself with a chuckle as I struggled with the paraphernalia.

When I entered the social hall, my eyes immediately searched for Phil, and it did not take me long to locate him—surrounded by half a dozen admiring women. What really upset me was that he seemed to be enjoying the attention. For the most part, these were all married women, and I instinctively knew there was slight, if any, chance of their being interested in a love relationship with my husband. Even if they *had* been, Phil had his hands full with me already, and he was smart enough to know that. Why, then, had jealousy loomed its ugly head like this?

I put the incident out of my mind until one day when I was sharing some of my experiences with a group of diaconate wives. As I related it to them, a woman in her sixties nodded in agreement. In fact, she was so excited she could not contain herself. "I know just what you mean," she said. "Almost exactly the same thing happened to me."

My personal encounter with envy made me more determined than ever to keep the romance in our marriage and our relationship growing. In that way, if any woman should become interested in Phil, I would not feel threatened by her.

Trusting had now found its way into our lives as deacons' wives—trusting not only in respect to other women but also in another important aspect of our husbands' ministries—confidentiality. Phil was sometimes called upon to hear some very personal concerns. At times he, in effect, heard someone's "confession" before that person went to a priest to receive the graces of the sacrament of reconciliation. These concerns, when related to him, were obviously meant for my husband's ears alone. Therefore, if others were going to feel comfortable confiding in Phil, they needed to feel certain that he would not repeat what they had said—not even to me. Until ordination, we had been a couple in the habit of sharing almost everything, so I was not particularly fond of being separated from even this small part of Phil's life. But taking a good look at my own life, I realized that I, too, had friends who confided in me, and there were times when I was not free to repeat a word, not even to Phil.

Adopting an attitude of "What the Lord wants me to know, he'll make sure I find out. The rest is not important" made it much easier to accept the fact that my role as confidant sometimes required asking no questions and receiving no answers.

Apparently, trusting was an important part of the role I had been called upon to fulfill as Deacon Phil's wife because the more completely I trusted my deacon, the more I was able to let go of some of my claim to him. As Mrs. Phil Mraz, I suppose I had been rather possessive of the attention my husband paid me as well as of the time for the things we did together. However, as the wife of Deacon Phil Mraz, I found that I needed to let go of some of my claim to Phil's time and attention as well as to recognize the fact that some of the energy he had previously expended in doing things with me and our family was now rightfully directed elsewhere.

At his ordination I had experienced a strange sense of loss when Phil had left our pew to take his place at the altar. At that time I had instinctively known I had given part of Phil back to God for ministry in the Church. In my mind he was still "my deacon," and even after I had stated that I was giving him freely to the Lord for ministry, I found that from time to time I wanted to take all of him back.

"There are many times when I would prefer to have my husband home with me rather than off ministering to others," one deacon's wife related. "There are many occasions when I miss having him sit with me in the pew—especially at church functions where I see so many other couples sitting together. How I would like to have him at my side for our parish's traditional renewal of marriage vows when all around me couples are holding hands as they renew their vows in front of their smiling children. But if I happen to attend the same Mass as my husband that day, I have to be content with our eyes meeting above the heads of those in the pews that separate us as we renew our commitment to each other."

"It's one thing for a woman to let a child go, but it's an entirely different matter when you let your husband go. It's a little frightening, sometimes lonesome, sometimes irritating, and many times inconvenient," another related.

Gradually, relinquishing some, but not all, of my personal claim became easier. Surprisingly, my not clinging to my husband or holding him to me produced a chain reaction of happenings; the more freedom Phil had, the more I received from him—his love, his admiration, and his sharing of himself with me. As I let go of some of my possessiveness and overprotectiveness, he was able to minister with a greater self-confidence and a new sense of freedom. Actually, Phil needed me to be his freedom giver in order to grow and become more and more the deacon God was calling him to be. In trusting and letting go, I had acquired another new role—that of enabler.

Helping Phil to vest at ordination had been an outward sign of my support of his work for the Church and of my willingness to aid him in whatever ways I could, but little had I known at ordination all that life as the deacon's wife would entail.

My list of roles was much longer than I had ever imagined it would be: Wife, Lover, Companion, Best friend, Homemaker, Health counselor, Diaconate teammate, Private secretary, Protector, Teacher, Toughest critic, Ministry consultant, Loyal fan, Family focuser, Family barometer, Foot stomper, Cheerleader, Prayer partner, Prayer support, Team manager, Quiet support, Truster, Confidant, Freedom giver, Enabler.

As Phil's wife I suppose I had always been all of these things to him. But somehow, along with ordination had come increased needs on Phil's part and a heightened awareness of those needs on my part. Viewed separately, each addition to my former wifely role appeared small and insignificant; most of the additions had made their way into my life without my even realizing it. However, when added together, the assorted tasks were taking considerably more of my time and energy than I had expected or realized, for each involved work of some sort—physical, mental, or emotional—time-consuming work. Each of the tasks involved had served to make my already busy life even more complicated by adding to my constantly changing list of personal responsibilities.

"A woman's life is an ever-changing experience, to my thinking much more so than a man's life," another wife shared. "Almost every life experience we have as a married couple has more impact on the woman than the man." Comments such as these from other deacons' wives have helped to support my theory that when a man is ordained, in many, but not all cases, his wife is the one who finds herself with so many additional obligations and concerns that she often leads a more stress-filled life than her husband.

An article in a national diaconal publication gives further evidence to support my suspicion. The deacons and their wives attending a workshop on burnout at an annual regional diaconate conference in Denver answered sixteen questions in a self-rating Clergy Burnout Inventory. Of the sixty-five deacons who took advantage of the inventory, 20 percent discovered they were experiencing some degree of burnout in their lives. However, of the forty-nine wives who answered the same questions, almost 35 percent had scores which indicated they were experiencing various degrees of burnout. Nearly 15 percent more women than men were suffering from symptoms of burnout.

The figures of those scoring in the extreme burnout range provided even more conclusive proof to support my hypothesis. Only one man, but *seven* of the women, scored in that range. One and a half percent of the men versus 14 3/16 percent of the women were extremely burned out.*

The published results of the workshop's inventory supported my suspicion that many of the wives were having more difficulty than their husbands in living peacefully with the busyness and stress the diaconate had brought into their lives. It also proved that many other wives, not just those in our diocese, have felt pressures similar to those which I had experienced. While we tend to focus on the men in the diaconate and all they are encountering, perhaps there should also be some attention paid to what is happening to the wives.

At Phil's ordination when our bishop had cautioned the men that their ministries would be accompanied by suffering, had he known that we wives would suffer, too? Although the suffering had not always seemed worth it at the time, all I went through in adjusting to my role as a deacon's wife was worthwhile. The extra work, the stress, and the emotional struggles involved in my acceptance of each of the areas in which I was ministering to my husband had led to a tremendous amount of personal growth on my part.

*See David Balk, "Burnout and the Permanent Diaconate: Threat to Ministry, Opportunity for Grace," *Diaconal Quarterly x*, no. 1 (Winter 1984) 13-24.

Although on the surface I seemed to be the same woman who had tagged along when her husband had been accepted into the formation program, because the diaconate had caused so many changes in our lives, I knew it could not possibly have left me untouched. Perhaps in exploring what it meant to be a deacon's wife, I needed to do some reflecting on the woman in her own right, too.

8

The Woman Who Is a Deacon's Wife

Describing the woman, the unique being who is married to a deacon is a challenge. First, one needs to know that in this particular group of women no two are alike.

Deacons' wives come in all ages, sizes, shapes, and colors. Each woman comes to her diocesan diaconate program equipped with her individual personality, temperament, talents, ideas, needs, hopes, and fears. Moreover, her husband, her marriage, her family, and her ministry are different from those of all the others. Every deacon's wife is her own person. There is a beauty in that, for each brings her individuality as well as her past life experience to enrich not simply the program and the lives of those within it but her husband's ministry as well. As diverse as we women are, the part the diaconate plays in our lives as women in our own right and the way it affects the core of our being is naturally very different for each one of us.

Yet, strangely enough, as diversified as we are, overall we deacons' wives seem to have much in common. To begin with, we ladies generally have a deep love for our spouses, take pride in their accomplishments, and wish to support them and their endeavors in any way in which we are able. Without that strong, loving commitment, we would never have agreed to our husbands' applying for admission to the diaconate program in the first place. We also have enough faith and trust in our husbands to allow them the freedom to take on additional responsibilities and accept new challenges. As wives, we have a strong commitment to our spouses, to our marriages, and, for those of us who have children, to our families.

However, being secure in our marriages and in our family life is only the beginning. One of the Cleveland diaconate staff members has said that deacons' wives are prayerful women. On the whole, we seem to have developed an ever-deepening faith and trust in the Lord. Our prayer life and our spiritual growth are generally as important to us as our desire to do the will of God. But we are not isolated in our own spiritual life, for each of us has shared our faith with our spouse and with our family even before becoming a part of the diaconate community.

It is our faith which has helped to make us aware of an important fact. As women, *we* have not chosen to become a part of the diaconate and involved in our husbands' ministries—*God* has chosen us. "Before I formed you in the womb I knew you/before you were born I dedicated you . . ." (Jer 1:5). This first reading from Phil's ordination Mass is just as appropriate for those who are deacons' wives as it is for the deacons themselves because we, too, have been called by God to fulfill a special role. Before we were born, the Lord dedicated us to be the helpmates of his deacons. Throughout our lives, our heavenly Father gently shaped and prepared us as he slowly led us to our respective husbands and eventually, with them, to the diaconate.

As deacons' wives, we not only received our own unique call to the diaconate, but we also went through the necessary application process. Whether we listened to tapes of classes, actually attended sessions with our spouses, proofread papers, or simply lifted our husbands' spirits, we wives shared in our husbands' time of preparation and of ordination, too.

But support and encouragement for our husbands' involvements did not end with ordination, for supporting and encouraging them have generally become a way of life for us. It seems that after an initial period of adjustment, we have found ourselves with an even deeper commitment to our spouses and to their ministries. Ministry has become so important to us, in fact, that we have willingly taken on some of the household responsibilities which once belonged to our husbands. Out of necessity we have also become flexible in our scheduling of daily activities which allows us to live fairly peacefully with our sometimes hectic life-styles. All of this involves a sincere desire to share our deacons with others through their individual diaconal ministries.

During our husbands' time in formation, we wives had been busy, too. As their helpmates we had been learning, growing, and discovering more about ourselves, about our faith, and about the ordained ministry to which our particular deacon candidate was being called. On the whole, growth of all kinds continues to be important to us. Forever growing and changing, not one of us is the same person now that we were yesterday, nor is our experience of the diaconate the same for us today as it was last week. Undoubtedly, with the passage of time, the important role we have as deacons' wives and women in our own right will continue to unfold for each of us as we continue to discover exactly who it is God is calling us to be.

To date, other than that there should be certainty about a wife's consent, her blameless Christian life, and the qualities that will not impede or bring dishonor on her husband's ministry,* there have been no real guidelines for the selection of the women who are the deacons' wives. Each individual diocesan diaconate staff most likely has its own general list of things it looks for in the wife of each of its applicants. It would be impossible for any program to be

---

*See the apostolic letter of Pope Paul VI, June 18, 1967, *General Norms for Restoring the Permanent Diaconate in the Latin Church* (Washington: United States Catholic Conference, 1967) 5.

too specific, however, without producing all-of-a-kind women. How dull that would be. Loving, committed, faith-filled, excited about growing, flexible—these attributes would be desirable, but other than that, the only rule which could possibly be applied is that we deacons' wives should feel free to be, in fact *need* to be, ourselves—unique, one-of-a-kind women.

Without a doubt, each deacon's wife the world over is unique in her own way. Each one will always be different from the others, yet at the same time, she will always be very much like them.

As one of those unique women, I certainly did not feel any different from the way I had been before we applied for admission to the diaconate program. Yet I knew I was not the same, for on the inside, a remarkable transforma-tion had taken place—a transformation caused by much per-sonal growth.

Becoming a part of the diaconate had caused me to be very busy—busier than I had ever been before. I was so busy, in fact, that I had pains in my chest and arm for a short time not long after Phil's ordination, pains caused by stress—stress caused by living a complicated diaconate and lay life-style. Those physical manifestations of tension were a blessing in disguise. In attempting to overcome them, I was forced to take a good look at myself and at the way I was living.

As one who had for years been more concerned with meeting the needs of others than admitting I had some needs of my own, I was now confronted with the fact that in order for me to live peacefully with the diaconate as a woman in my own right and to successfully fulfill my role as a woman, wife, and mother for the many years I envi-sioned yet to come, I would have to begin to take reason-ably good care of myself. The only way in which I would be able to do that would be by looking after my physical, social, emotional, and spiritual well-being. These were the very same concerns I had as Phil's health counselor, but

I seemed to have overlooked them in regard to myself. Learning to realistically, unselfishly take care of myself was not easy, for being in tune with my own needs and working to satisfy them required numerous adjustments in my thinking as well as in my actions.

Eating right, getting enough rest and sufficient exercise, and spending time with my friends were all important in helping me to relax and to refresh myself and my outlook on life. At the same time they helped to control some of the tension which had led to the physical signs of stress in my life. However, if I were going to be really good to myself, some additional adjustments were necessary.

In order to remain emotionally healthy, the first fact I had to face was that as a woman who was a deacon's wife, it was not going to be easy to be a woman in my own right at the same time. There was a real danger of becoming so caught up in who my husband was and what he was about, I could easily have lost my self-identity entirely. Although I may have spent considerable time ironing my husband's long white alb, I could not afford to hide behind it by being known *only* as the deacon's wife. Phil and I were two very different, distinct individuals called by God to do his will—each in our own way. Even though it would probably have been easier to have been simply the deacon's wife rather than to have to make my own way, that would have been avoiding who I was and who God was calling me to be.

The most obvious way of making sure I would always be myself was to maintain my own interests and to cultivate new ones. Not only did these activities add a little sparkle to my life, but they also helped me to discover a wealth of ever-unfolding gifts and talents uniquely my own. A ministry especially suited to me seemed to be unfolding right before my eyes, too—a ministry distinctly different from that of my husband. Who would ever have guessed that diaconal involvement could be so instrumental in helping a woman to develop a greater appreciation of herself and of her ability to make her own contribution to the universe?

In order to hold on to the new self-confidence which was developing within me, continued growth was necessary. But that growth could only come about if I were able to let go of some of the perfectionist in me and begin to accept the gift of my humanness. As much as I would have liked God to change my human condition, it did not appear that he was about to; therefore, I had no choice. Changing was up to me. For my well-being, I was going to have to accept myself just as I was—fully human and far from perfect.

Here, I was called upon to let go of some of the unrealistic expectations I had placed upon myself in trying to be the ideal wife and mother. With a little determination, I was finding it easier to feed my family more simply and to overlook some of the clutter which comes along with a family of savers. Having more realistic expectations helped me to slow down a bit giving me more time to listen to the peace of the early morning and to laugh and play with family and friends.

However, becoming comfortable with the fact that I was a mere mortal was going to require some additional accepting. Following Phil's ordination, I discovered people were watching my husband. His life had entered the public domain. Surprisingly, many of those who knew I was the deacon's wife were watching me, too. Some had gone so far as to place me on a pedestal. At Phil's ordination I had been hurt by the lack of recognition I had received from others. Now it was actually a relief to be Phil's quiet, almost-invisible support most of the time. In that way, only a small percentage of the parishioners would know who I was. Having to give up my privacy, something I valued highly, was one aspect of the diaconate on which I had not counted, and living a fishbowl existence for the rest of my life was definitely not something to which I was looking forward.

Now it was time for me to let go of the subtle pressures I had unknowingly been placing upon myself following

Phil's ordination—the pressures to perform as a deacon's wife should and to be someone others could admire. Who did that someone have to be? It could only be me, just me— no play acting, no putting on airs. I was realizing once again, just as I had when Phil and I had first applied to the program, that all I could ever be was me, not perfect, very human, me. When I stopped to think about it, "me" was the woman who had been called to be the deacon's wife in the first place, and doing my best was all anyone, including myself, had the right to expect of me.

There was a wonderful sense of freedom in knowing that it was not only okay but also necessary to be myself, and I needed that freedom not simply for myself but for the community around me as well. If our Church had ordained Phil, a married man who was less than perfect, who had a wife who was less than perfect, then it only made sense that it was okay for others to be less than perfect, too. In accepting my humanness, I was indirectly helping others to do the same. Now, all I had to do was to practice living comfortably with my new-found freedom. It was not long, however, before I was put to the test.

A committee of parishioners investigating the feasibility of installing a new full-sized pipe organ for our parish church had decided to recommend the purchase. When the proposal for acquiring the organ was presented to the liturgy commission of which I was a member, I found myself in a delicate position.

Since our old electronic organ was serviceable, I was certain there were more important things our parish could do with the money. Yet as Deacon Phil's wife, I was afraid that voicing my opinion might jeopardize his standing with the parish community, the organ committee, the organist, the choir, or the parish staff, especially our pastor. At the first sign of strife, my new-found freedom to be myself seemed to have disappeared.

After I weighed the possible effects of expressing my thoughts, I knew that I would eventually be disappointed with myself if I remained quiet, so I spoke out against the purchase, which was eventually approved despite my opposition. Fortunately, with time, it did not seem that I had harmed Phil or his ministry in any way. Our pastor did not treat either Phil or me any differently than he had before, and as far as I knew, there were no adverse comments from parishioners. Even our parish organist, who had been my staunch opponent on the issue, simply smiled when I asked him how my position had affected his relationship with my husband. "Well, as far as I'm concerned, everyone is entitled to their own incorrect opinion," he said.

Nevertheless, it would always be good for me to weigh an issue before speaking out on it. As a deacon's wife, I would always be in a delicate position where parish issues were concerned, yet within the framework of that position, I would still need the freedom to be me.

Ever becoming more and more what God was calling me to be, I had certainly been making strides in the personal growth department. My intellectual and spiritual development were two important aspects of that growth. The Christian Family Movement and our parish renewal program had given me nudges in the right direction even before our diaconal involvement had further stimulated my interest in learning.

During formation, I had been spoon-fed growth when I had listened to Phil's tapes and had taken advantage of the numerous faith experiences available. Now, as the wife of an ordained deacon, I wanted all the knowledge and personal growth I could possibly acquire not only to support my deacon husband and his ministry, but also, and just as importantly, for myself because I had a deep desire to continue to know my God and to develop my relationship with him more fully.

With so much to accomplish each day, a specific time for my personal growth often seemed a luxury I could not afford. As a result, my spiritual growth was minimal. For the most part I was trying to run on the spiritual fill-up I had received during formation. No wonder I was beginning to feel drained. My new spirituality was obviously not working for me.

Fortunately, the diaconate program had not left me completely stranded; the installations, ordinations, annual couples' retreat, and days of recollection for the wives offered growth experiences tailor-made for those of us in the program. I needed these diaconal growth opportunities more than I had realized, for the spiritual functions at our parish or within the framework of our C.F.M. involvement were no longer meeting the deep spiritual hunger I had unknowingly developed, nor were they taking into account my seminary training.

But following Phil's ordination, I could no longer count on the program to painlessly provide all of my growth in faith. Taking advantage of every opportunity for spiritual growth, spending quiet time in prayer at home daily, doing spiritual reading, meeting regularly with a confessor and a spiritual director, and spending time away from our busy life-style at a day of recollection and an annual retreat were essential for my ever-changing growth in faith. All these activities involved time spent with my Lord—time followed by honest effort, self-discipline, and a sharing of myself. Eventually, by using the hours in each day to grow closer to God, life itself became a prayer.

While struggling with Phil through our painful period of adjustment following ordination, I had found myself wondering just what I was doing in the program. Was I a deacon's wife for Phil's sake or my own self-satisfaction, or was I doing all of this for God? With time, I had come to know that, although his desire to be a deacon had certainly played a part in my decision, I was not involved in the diaconate solely for Phil, and I certainly was not involved in supporting my husband to impress others or for my personal gain. A whole list of various ways to achieve personal satisfaction would be easy for me to compile without my having to mention the diaconate. It had become obvious that my commitment to the diaconate was primarily because of a deep love for the Lord and a desire to do his will.

Much growth—spiritual and intellectual—had occurred, along with an increasing awareness of the need to stay physically, socially, and emotionally healthy. So much had happened within me as a result of my having become a part of the diaconate and of its having become a part of me. Deciding just what had prompted the growth which our diaconal involvement had caused in the core of my being was not easy until the now-familiar words "communication" and "priorities" came to mind.

Communication for me as a woman meant keeping in touch with myself, with God, and with my family as well as with the others in my life. In so doing I found I was discovering much more about myself than I could ever have learned alone. That was important, for in discovering who I was and who I was becoming, I realized that some semblance of order in my personal life was essential.

Largely because of my experience in the diaconate, I had come to know that my relationship with God had to be at the top of my priorities, for my relationship with the Lord was the glue which held all the aspects of my existence together. Next in order of importance came my own well-being so that I would be able to take care of the other things on my list. Phil's well-being and that of the children, my marriage and daily relationships, my household duties, and my outside activities—including ministry—followed, in that order. Yet setting realistic goals for myself had taught me that each priority had to be addressed in terms of what was most important at any given moment in order to have a balance in my day-to-day living and peace within me.

Each deacon's wife is a woman in her own right, a wife, and a diaconate helpmate in her own way. Most often, her life is further complicated with the additional role of mother. There are many facets of her life all able to be compartmentalized yet woven into the fabric of her being in such a way that they can not be separated. Each woman, a unique package deal, in effect married her Church when her husband was ordained.

In accepting my role as deacon's helpmate, I had reached the point where it was now a natural, normal part of my womanly existence. I actually needed it to make my life complete, yet I knew I was still just Dottie, a woman emerging, growing, and learning more about herself, continuing the search for the still partially hidden treasure of her gifts and talents, and looking to the future with a sense of anxious anticipation while trying to become more and more the best person she could be according to God's plan for her. I had become a woman attempting to meet the tension-laden challenges of life head-on while realizing that stress was not always bad for me because it was causing much personal growth. All of this was helping to free me to become more and more a woman with an honest feeling of self-worth and a woman who had acquired some sense of personal satisfaction with herself and with her life.

I do not want to give the impression, even for a moment, that I had it "all together." I definitely did not. Nor did I deliberately set out to change and grow. I had simply, naturally, sometimes painfully, sometimes joyfully adapted to the needs I saw—most of the time without even realizing it. It is only in retrospect that I can see how much I have grown.

At a recent ordination, the bishop told the men being ordained, "You will be radically different when you leave here. You will receive the Spirit of God. You will be changed and transformed, but it is only a beginning. You will be transformed daily."

How right the bishop was. I had witnessed that change taking place in my husband. A similar transformation had taken place within me—a transformation that had made me radically different. Since I was a changed woman married to a transformed man, it would only be natural that there would be some changes in our children and in our family life, too.

9

The Deacon's Family

Since our diaconal involvement had such far-reaching effects on both Phil and me, it would have been foolish to think that it would not have affected our children also. Had anyone other than our children been a member of our household, they, too, would have found it impossible to remain unaffected.

What Phil and I wanted for our offspring, above all else, was that they be able to enjoy a normal childhood in spite of the fact that their father was ordained. We were determined to protect our children from any problems—physical, social, emotional, or spiritual—which might develop because of our Church involvement.

From the first, our marriage, our children, and our family life were of prime importance to us. Until the diaconate program entered our lives, our actions had generally indicated that. However, the rigid schedule of classes and our expected presence at diaconal meetings and functions during formation and then our enthusiasm for ministry immediately following ordination had often reversed that order for us. Even when Phil and I had finally reached the point where we felt we had the diaconate under control in our lives, diaconal ministry still had an uncanny way of slipping into our schedule and taking over when we were not watching.

The diaconate would always reside with us, but if we succeeded in raising our children to be the happy, well-adjusted, free-to-be-themselves, independent, faith-filled adults we hoped they would someday be, they would eventually be moving out on their own. Our primary responsibility lay in raising the children whom God had entrusted to us before he called us to the diaconate. If in the name of ministry, we should accomplish many good works that touched the lives of a multitude of God's people, but, in the process, lost our children because we had not first ministered to their needs, we would have lost what was most important of all.

No one else—no grandparent, friend, or babysitter, no matter how loving or special—could take our place in creating the warm childhood memories we wanted for our children. That was up to us. To Phil and me, a normal childhood for our offspring meant our being loving parents who cared enough to listen, to teach, to discipline, to spend time with, and to play with our children so that they might mature secure in our love with the knowledge that they were of the utmost importance to us. It also meant allowing them to develop their individual interests and natural talents, knowing they had our loving, concerned support in all their endeavors. It meant spending time with each child and coming to know him or her as an individual while each child came to know us in that way, too. It sometimes meant being available to our children when they really needed us day or night no matter what else was going on at the time. It always meant being alert to our children's needs as well as following through with appropriate actions on all the needs we perceived, spoken and unspoken.

Phil's ordination had in no way made us a super family. Diaconate or not, our household was still a living symbol of humanness, and our lives were filled with the reality of day-to-day family living. The relationships to build and to maintain; the house, the yard, the cars to care for; and the never-ending bills to be paid were all very real. The everyday sounds emitting from our household proved that our family was very much the same as the others we knew.

"Mom, could you wash my jeans for tonight?" I thought I had done all the wash there was. Where had these jeans been hiding?

"I need a ride to practice." Maybe we should just leave the car idling and ready to go.

"There's nothing *good* to eat in this house." But I just grocery shopped two days ago!

For the most part, the diaconate had not altered our youngsters' comments or our thoughts as parents much at all. The same was true for most of the comments Phil and I were making to our children.

"Your closet is clean. How about working on the rest of the room?"

"Anyone for a game of catch after supper?"

"Good night. God bless you and keep you safe."

Sound familiar? For anyone with children, our family still seemed what one might term normal.

Because our diaconal commitment had made it known from the first that it was also going to demand a fair amount of self-sacrifice from each one of us as well as from our family as a whole, Phil and I wanted to be sure that the diaconate would not tear us apart. Family activities were of prime importance to us, for our experience proved that working, playing, celebrating, and praying together were invaluable in insuring that we would continue to draw closer as a family. Scheduling a weekly family night, taking advantage of celebrations built into the Church year, and developing new family traditions as well as maintaining the old ones helped our family to grow closer in relationships and in faith.

Attending Sunday Mass regularly as a family was nearly impossible, and on those occasions when all family members attended the same Mass, we seldom sat together. What with two boys serving, a child attending pre-school Sunday school, and a deacon assisting at the altar and distributing Communion to parish shut-ins, there were some Sunday mornings when we were fortunate to see each other at all. The altar table, the very thing which was bringing other families together, was separating the Mraz family at church. That made Phil and me all the more determined to see that our family was at least gathered around the table at home each Sunday for an informal brunch planned for whenever the last of our commitments for the morning was completed. Time, menu, even the family members who did the cooking, all varied, but the brunch was considered essential.

Actually, the activities our family adopted in self-defense enriched our lives—an unexpected bonus provided by our new commitment. However, there was an even greater bonus, for Phil's diaconal ministry itself was enriching our family life by giving it a new sense of meaning and purpose.

Of course, some of the ministry my husband performed—adult programs and counseling, for instance—could only be done by him alone; however, even here the children and I were able to support him with our prayers. But it was amazing the number of ways in which our whole family found ourselves naturally becoming involved in the work Phil was doing. It was not unusual to see our children helping to put the deacon's chair away after Mass, or to see us leaving church with one child proudly carrying Dad's lectionary and another his stole. Furthermore, by participating together in more extensive ministry involvements by accompanying their dad when he distributed Communion to shut-ins or by collecting toys for distribution to those less fortunate, our children were being given numerous opportunities to experience the uplifting, fulfilling feeling which comes with sharing yourself when doing something out of the ordinary for others. In giving of ourselves as a family, we were being drawn closer by the services we performed together.

It was not simply the family times we were working so

hard to maintain or the ministry we were involved in with Phil which were uniting us. The diaconate program was doing its share by providing us with numerous new faith experiences and opportunities for family growth and growth in faith. By attending the installations and ordination ceremonies, our family experienced a whole new aspect of our Church together. The diaconate Christmas party, the summer picnic, the family formation weekend, and the cluster get-togethers provided social time and encouraged friendships with others who shared our faith commitment. Here were friends with whom our youngsters could feel free to discuss the diaconate, should they ever feel the need.

I sometimes shudder to think of what could have happened to our household had Phil and I not learned to keep our priorities in order. In an attempt to offset the diaconate busyness and to make sure our family remained our first priority, Phil and I had been forced to develop and maintain effective means to preserve our family unit. Fortunately for us all, our determination and hard work had paid off in benefits which far outweighed any disadvantages the diaconate had brought into our lives. By deliberately providing plenty of quality family time, by sharing ministry with our children, and by taking advantage of the opportunities for family enrichment provided by the program itself, our family was growing *together*.

In many ways our children's lives resembled those of their peers. Yet their lives were no longer the same as the lives of their friends in our neighborhood. Our children no longer had typical parents. Phil and I had not only totally committed ourselves to being open to the will of God, but had also promised before a church filled with people to live up to that commitment for the rest of our lives. Dad was a deacon. No one else in our neighborhood or, at that time, in our entire city of nearly one hundred thousand people, had a dad who assisted the priest at the altar at Mass—complete with alb and stole. No one else's father preached, baptized, officiated at weddings and wake services, or assisted the bishop at special ceremonies. At cub scout pack meetings, where Dad had once taken his turn presiding as cub master, he was now spiritual director—a role previously held by one of the parish priests. None of the other children in our neighborhood had a father who could do that as an ordained clergyman. Not only that, but our children had been deepening their own individual relationships with the Lord and, because of our diaconal involvement, had had the opportunity for many more faith experiences than their friends.

How did they feel about all of this? There was only one way to know for sure, and that was to ask them. Our children had shared their comments on the diaconate with us from time to time, but for this book I wanted to get a broader picture of what it means to be a deacon's kid. I asked some of the children of other deacons in our diocese what they found to be both the *advantages* and *disadvantages* of having a deacon dad. Their answers included not only stories of their pride and joy but also an honest account of some of the difficulties they had encountered in adjusting to the diaconate as well.

Mark, age thirteen, told me that in the beginning having his father gone to class twice a week was hard. "But because I knew what my dad was doing, it was okay. I really got into it with the family weekend, the cluster program, and the parties where I made a lot of new friends," Mark told me. "It was a good feeling being around the people my dad was ordained with—the people who went through the same stuff we did. Then when he was ordained and I watched him distribute Communion, I would see peoples' faces light up when they received from him. I was really proud, and I would think 'That's my dad up there!' "

From toddler to those in their twenties, all with whom I spoke were proud of their fathers. Our Andy, who was nineteen months old at the time of Phil's ordination, had referred to Phil as his "Church Dad" on Sundays and would ask as we waited for Mass to begin, "Is Daddy going to be a deacon now?"

One young woman in her early twenties told me the fact that her father was a deacon gave her a sense of pride in who *she* was as a person, too. "I don't go around telling people about Dad—bragging about him or anything," she told me, "but when someone pays him a compliment, I am proud to be able to say 'That's my dad!'"

One deacon's wife told me that she had been concerned at first because her daughter had been using the diaconate as a status symbol among her friends, but when having an ordained father became a way of life, the daughter simply found it a source of personal pride.

However, the feeling was not always one of pride.

"When my dad was ordained, I was in the seventh grade, and I was embarrassed when he assisted at our parochial school Masses. By the time I was in the eighth grade I was so used to it that it didn't bother me anymore. Now that I'm a high school junior, it's just normal for Dad to be a deacon," Joe told me.

How did the deacons' kids feel about their fathers' ministries?

"I liked going with Dad when he distributed Communion to the shut-ins. It felt good to be with him, and the people we visited became my friends," our daughter Kathy told me. "I liked seeing him assist at the altar, but the part I liked best was listening to his homilies. Sometimes, but not very often, he used examples from our family life. I was always a little afraid he might use my name, but he never did. Hearing people congratulate him after a good homily was great!"

Of her own accord, one teenage girl asked her friends for their reactions to her dad's homilies and then relayed the information to her father.

For faith-oriented families, there seem to be some advantages to being the deacons' kids.

"My dad's a big help with my religion homework," Beth, a high school senior, told me.

"Not many kids have parents who can answer their questions about God like Dad," Bob said. "And I know some bishops, priests, and sisters better than most of my friends do."

"I decided to become a server because of my dad. It was neat when I got to serve and my dad was deacon for the bishop at the same Mass," Mark related. "I've enjoyed being exposed to so many different things, like ordinations. I think I'm more spiritually mature than my eighth-grade friends because of all that I have experienced."

There seemed to be many advantages to having a deacon in the house—advantages not merely for the deacon and his wife but for their children as well. However, there was another concern—a concern for the social well-being of the deacons' offspring. How were the friends of the children in the diaconate reacting to all of this? How were the youngsters in the program coping with their peers' reactions?

"It feels good when your friends say 'Hey, I saw your dad at Mass!'" one young teenage boy remarked.

Several children were surprised that their friends had asked them questions about the diaconate and about what it was like having a deacon for a dad.

"My dad seems to be able to maintain a balance," Dave, a college sophomore remarked. "He's not overly pious; he's real human. My friends enjoy being with him and sometimes come over just to talk to him. Dad knows how to laugh and joke and have a good time with us, but he doesn't get too carried away."

"My dad works with the youth at our parish," Beth told me. "But he won't work on the teen retreat I'm helping with. He's afraid I'll be uncomfortable with him around, and I think I might be. My father's looking out for my best interests, and I appreciate it."

Many of the young people's comments showed not only that they admired their fathers but also that they expected much of their dads. After a heated argument with his teenage daughter early one Sunday morning, one deacon was feeling so low that he thought about giving up his diaconal ministry. Certainly the last thing he felt like doing was preaching at Mass later that morning. But the deacon had made a commitment to preach, and the priests at his parish were counting on him. As miserable as he was, the deacon assisted at Mass that morning and preached as scheduled.

"I would have been disappointed in you if you hadn't gone. I would have thought you were a phony," his daughter told him later.

The deacons' kids interviewed seemed well aware of the deep, lifetime commitment their parents had made to their faith. They were also realistic about the disadvantages involved.

"I like my dad helping other people, but I don't like it when he's gone *too* much," one thirteen-year-old said. "I like him spending time with me, too! Sometimes I feel torn because I miss having my father sit with our family at Mass. But I really like to see him assist at the altar, and I want my dad to be happy and to do good for others. Sometimes I feel selfish because I want more time with him."

"I've seen a lot of pressure put on my dad," one boy remarked. "People seem to think he can do everything, and sometimes, he ends up feeling frustrated and yelling more at home."

"When Dad has time for the things he enjoys in addition to his ministry and time to be at home with us, too, he is more relaxed and our family life is better," another related. Although they may not have expressed priorities in quite the same manner as we adults had, these children had learned, from their own life experience, the value of keeping family first.

One of my main concerns from the time Phil had first mentioned the diaconate program had been that the deacons' children would find themselves with unreasonable expectations placed upon them simply because their fathers were part of the ordained clergy of the Church. Now it seemed that my concern had not been unfounded. The children interviewed were indeed feeling increased pressure in their lives—pressure from adults, from their peers, and from within themselves to be what deacons' kids "should be."

There was no doubt that our own children had extra pressure placed upon them from adults because, unfortunately, some of that pressure was coming from *me*. "They are the deacon's kids," I reasoned. "Others will expect them to be well behaved, especially in church." Yet, I tended to expect that of them, too. It was not only unrealistic to expect perfectly behaved children in church or anywhere else, but it was also contrary to the childhood Phil and I wanted for them. In any case the pressure I felt at first, and, in turn, sometimes placed upon our children was certainly very real.

I was not the only one who expected much of the deacon's kids; some of their dads were overdoing it, too. One child declared he did not like it when his dad pushed him too hard or attempted to push him to be something he was not ready to be.

But pressure from adults was not coming solely from home. "You should know better than to do something like that. Your dad's a deacon!" one high school teacher scolded when a deacon's son had failed to live up to the standards set for him in the teacher's mind.

"People know you because your dad's a deacon. People who didn't know me very well thought I had to be perfect, especially some of the kids my age. They even told me so," Kathy shared. "Sometimes that put pressure on me, but I was just myself. I didn't care."

"My dad's a deacon, not me," another child explained, "I'm just me."

Surprisingly, even the pressure from within the children themselves had its positive aspects, at least from a parent's point of view. "Knowing that my father's a deacon has made me more responsible for my actions; I don't want to get thrown in jail,'' a nineteen-year-old boy told me.

Like their parents, the deacons' kids were experiencing added pressure from all sides, but on the surface at least, it certainly seemed that those with whom I spoke were handling the extra tension very well.

''The good definitely outweighed the bad,'' one youngster said. And this comment was supported by others.

''The diaconate has brought us closer as a family. Our family is special because our dad's a deacon.''

''Things didn't change when Dad became a deacon. He's still the same man he was before, and our family is still the same family that it has always been. Our parents would probably have brought us up the same way with or without the diaconate.''

It was impossible to talk with all of the children in our diocesan diaconate community. However, an in-depth study of the diaconate done here at the time of the tenth anniversary of the ordination of the first permanent deacon in our diocese served to substantiate the comments gathered.

Nearly one hundred of the deacons' offspring responded to a questionnaire designed especially for them; about 60 percent replied favorably to *all* aspects of the diaconate in their lives. Five percent responded negatively overall, an indication that they were having a problem living comfortably with the diaconate, each for his or her own reasons. Perhaps it was simply some trouble with life in general which had prompted their negative attitudes. Since the questionnaires were unsigned, there was no way to know for sure. The remaining children answered with a combination of both positive and negative comments.

Because the remarks given the committee studying the diaconate were basically the same as those reported to me, I feel safe in labeling them universal, normal, okay diaconate feelings for the younger generation.

With few exceptions, the children of diaconate families seemed to be adjusting and handling things well and to be accepting their family's diaconal life-style. The overall expression was one of tremendous love and support for their fathers and their diaconal involvement. This fact coupled with an awareness of the diaconate's positive effects on both parents and children finally was able to put to rest my original fear that the children would suffer adversely from being the deacons' kids.

Knowing that our children were adjusting to the diaconate well was freeing for Phil and me. The children's acceptance of their father's diaconal ministry as a way of life helped us to attain a sense of inner peace and confidence which allowed us to be better parents and more effective ministers at home and away.

Just as the bishop had said the men in the program would be transformed daily, we, as a family, were being changed and transformed daily in the light of Phil's ordination. That fact was especially noticeable in our family's ever-changing life-style and activities as the children grew. When the older children reached the teen years, they no longer viewed the diaconate in the same light as they had when our family joined the program. They were maturing and attempting to become more and more independent and free thinking, and that was good.

Since each member of our family and our family as a whole was continuously changing and growing, a constant and continuous evaluation of our family life was essential. Only by examining closely what was happening to our family life-style and by listening closely to what our children were saying about their experience of the diaconate were Phil and I able to discern whether or not diaconal ministry was causing continued growth at home or creating problems that would eventually tear our family apart.

To say that we always lived comfortably with Phil's ordained ministry would not be fair. It just was not true, for the Mraz family was still made up of seven very different, normal people who together were a normal family with the ups and downs of any normal family's day-to-day living.

There were many times, even after our adjustment period, when one or all of us was dissatisfied with our new life-style. As a family we struggled over and over again adjusting as our family grew spiritually, emotionally, and socially—together and as individuals.

However, to say that, for the most part, after an initial period of adjustment, our family was able to live together peacefully in spite of, and sometimes because of the diaconate, would be more accurate and definitely more honest. When all was said and done, the diaconate had been sampled, enjoyed, digested, and assimilated until it had become a natural, normal, integral part of our family life. For the most part it had, over a period of time, become a comfortable way of life for our household, just as it had for Phil, me, and each of our children as individuals. For us, it was good. Yet there could be no doubt that we were no longer the same family we had been before the diaconate had entered our lives, and now that we were different, tranformed, I could not help but wonder just how our faith-centered family and its members were fitting into the community around us.

10

Community—A Part Of, or Apart From?

How nice it would be to simply say that "the radically different deacon, his transformed wife and children, and his faith-centered family fit comfortably into the world around them with no problem at all." Unfortunately, life was not that simple following ordination.

Both Phil and I had been a part of many communities before the diaconate. In each group—our extended family, our friends, our neighbors, and those with whom we worked on the job or on parish-related projects—there were people who knew us and accepted us as we were, without reservation. Through the years, we had come to know the importance of these friends and of "belonging" for our personal affirmation, support, and growth.

Becoming a part of the diaconate program had not changed our basic human need for relationships or the fact that we were still a part of each of the communities we had been a part of before. Yet our diaconal involvement had somehow separated us from many people. Could an outsider have sensed our being apart? I doubt it. But the feeling of separation was real nonetheless. It was only by interviewing people from all areas of our life that I came to better understand that a combination of things had been responsible for a subtle, never really verbalized change in many of our relationships.

From the first, the legitimate concerns of family members and friends had begun to separate us. "Are you sure this is what you want to do?" "How does Dottie feel about the diaconate?" "How will Phil have the time for ministry?" we had been asked when informing others of our decision to apply. The fact that at that time none of us, not even Phil and I, knew for sure what the diaconate was all about had caused some added apprehension, too. Some family and friends admitted that they were afraid Phil's actions might cause them personal embarrassment, while others were afraid that our commitment might change us or that, because of it, they might lose us as friends.

Even after ordination, some were still hesitant to accept our involvement. "When I saw Phil at the altar at his Mass of Thanksgiving, I thought to myself, 'That's my brother up there. What does *he* know? How can he be up there preaching?' " one of my husband's brothers related. "But the more I saw Phil in his role as deacon, the more I realized he did have training. And the more I heard him preach, the more I realized he did have something to say from a working and family man's point of view related in a faith perspective."

Here, time had become our friend. With time, those who knew us saw that, on the whole, my husband's ministry was being well received by our parish and, although our family was busy, our priorities were in order. Eventually, most of those who knew us began to relax and take pride in our commitment.

Pride became a force that was strengthening some of our old friendships. Yet, in spite of the pride others had in us, there were things in addition to their original concerns which caused the subtle separation between us. Admiration was one.

Apparently, a respect for Phil as "clergy" had caused some of our friends to stand back in awe at our commitment. Since my husband seldom wore his collar and did not seem to be carried away with himself or his ministry, this new respect was surprising. Here again, time was the answer to the barriers others had erected. As our family and friends saw that we were basically the same as we had always been, that we still knew how to laugh and have fun, and that we were not about to force our faith upon them, they began to relax in our presence once again.

However, even after the concerns had quieted and the awe had died away, it became obvious that our busy lifestyle was responsible for a strain on some of our relationships.

"With the onset of the diaconate, you were still friends, but you weren't as available as you had been before," one friend shared. "That bothered me. I thought that you just didn't want to be bothered with us anymore. It was as though you had forgotten the people you had left behind."

Left behind? Phil and I had certainly never meant to give anyone that impression. If even one person among all of those interviewed had mentioned any negative changes they had seen in us or in our attitudes, I would have admitted to our using the diaconate as a status symbol. But that was not the case. "Phil and you are always just you," one woman related. From others, the words I heard mentioned over and over were "growth," "dedication," "commitment," "more out-going"—all positives.

Why then, had some felt left behind? From the time the diaconate had entered our lives, we had been busy. But could we rightly blame the diaconate alone for the difficulty we were having finding time to be with friends? A good look at our lives and at the lives of other friends and relatives provided the answers needed to ease the sick feeling that had developed in the pit of my stomach when I heard my friend's comment.

First, few of the people we knew had as many children as we had. Unfortunately, we had apparently failed to explain that combining the busyness of a good-sized young family and ministry left little time for anything else.

Furthermore, our weekends were often busy with ministry commitments made up to as much as six months or a year in advance. Anyone attempting to get together with us would often hear, "I'm sorry. We already have a diaconate event scheduled then." At times, it had been easier to say, "That week is really busy. Let's try for another" and allow others to assume it was because of the diaconate rather than to explain that the children's activities, their childhood illnesses, family night, and other events were actually taking up more of our time than ministry. As a result, people blamed the diaconate for our unavailability. As unfair as that was, I could not very well chastise them for it, for the diaconate was our newest family involvement, and along with it had come the words "too busy."

However, there was more to our being unavailable than family priorities and ministry commitments. The diaconate had expanded our world to include many new friends. If we were to compare our social time with a pie divided, it only made sense that the greater the number of people sharing the pie, the smaller the piece for each of them. Because each of our friends, old and new alike, was important to us, Phil and I were not willing to give up any of them. Consequently, there was a smaller share of our time for each family member or old friend than there had been before the diaconate.

"I never thought about the new people in your lives or why I was feeling separated from you," one friend admitted. "All I knew was I resented feeling apart, and because of my resentment, I began to shun you. It had become a vicious circle. I can see now that I have been called upon to let go of some of my claim on your time and attention, but I wish we had talked about this sooner," our friend continued. So did I as I remembered the uncomfortable tension I had so often sensed when in this person's presence.

Fortunately, taking a realistic look at the lives of our family and friends was a help in dispelling any fear that our diaconate life-style was entirely to blame for the fact that we were not seeing as much of others. In talking with them, I could see that most of them were busier, had acquired new interests, and had made new friends, too. The same types of happenings seemed to be taking place in all of our lives. No wonder it was often difficult for us to get together.

However, since the part of my friend's comment which disturbed me the most was that she felt Phil and I had not wanted to be bothered with her, there was more soul-searching to be done. Could I honestly say there were *never* times when I had avoided getting together with others? No, I could not. Why had I sometimes pulled away from my friends?

First, there were times when Phil and I turned down invitations merely because we needed time to be with each other or with our children. Second, when feeling drained, being with others would often drain us further. That was especially true if those we were with subtly told us who we should be or expected us to minister to them in some way when what we really needed was to relax and to refresh ourselves. But understanding what our friends were feeling allowed us to make a concerted effort to accept invitations as well as to extend some of our own.

There was one additional matter which was separating us from those who had always been a part of our lives. It was something over which we had no control. Our diaconal involvement had caused a definite, invisible transformation to take place within each of us, and over a period of time, our lives had become more faith centered than world centered.

It was not that we had withdrawn from life or were so faith centered that we were ready to sell everything and follow Christ. This world was still important to us. We were very much a part of it. It was merely that, although we were still interested in worldly things and pleasures, they were no longer the most important things to us. As one deacon put it, "We are from this world, but not of this world. We see things differently than others see them." But there was more. We also had a vision of ministry and at least some idea of what God was calling us to do. Phil and I were the same persons we had always been now looking at life differently and aiming in a new direction, a direction which was different from that of most of the others in our lives.

Unfortunately, it was usually inappropriate for us to share much of what we felt and experienced with them. At most gatherings, the conversation was generally of a light, social nature. Even when the exchange of thoughts did turn to the Church, it was most often merely surface talk. Furthermore, when someone asked about Phil's ministry, rather than bore them with too many details, our answers were kept light and simple. Because Phil and I were not sharing the particulars of our faith commitment, most of those who had been a part of our lives for any length of time knew little about the extent of my husband's ministry or just what it involved for me and our children. In a very real way, our faith had come between us and many of our friends.

The people who probably came closest to understanding us and our life-style were those who had been working with us on Church projects. Although we shared some of our growth in faith and some of our diaconal experience with them from time to time and our growth certainly enriched our work with them tremendously, it was impossible, and here again actually inappropriate, to share everything.

Moreover, there was something new separating us from our committed lay friends. Even though they continued to be happy to have us working with them, there was an increased respect on their part for Phil, for his knowledge, and for his ordination as well as a new confidence in his abilities. Most of the groups we worked with were now looking to both of us as authority figures. Once merely members of a committee, we now often had a leadership role thrust upon us even if it was not an official position. In addition, some individuals began to look to Phil for spiritual help in the same manner in which they had always looked to priests for guidance, direction, and approval. These were the very people who had been a main source of support and encouragement for us in the past. They were our peers, yet they were now looking up to us when what Phil and I really needed was to feel free to relax and simply be ourselves with them.

It seemed that everywhere, our diaconal involvement had been responsible for an intangible separation between us and many of the people who had always been important to us. The concerns, resentment, and awe of our family and friends; our good-sized, busy family; the addition of new friends; our draining schedule; our growth in faith; the expanded experiences provided by the diaconate program; and our inability to share ourselves completely—there were many reasons for my feeling of isolation.

It is unfortunate that there are probably some who, no matter what is done to make things better, will never understand our family and our life-style or feel as close to us as they once did.

There are others who at first felt there was a cellophane barrier between us. We could see each other and touch lives by putting the palms of our hands together on either side of the divider; however, there was still something that remained between us and no longer allowed us to share everything and mingle freely. In some cases, openly talking about our feelings has helped us tear down and discard the barriers. In others, the cellophane remains, waiting to be removed.

Happily, there is a small group of family members and friends with whom there had been little sign of separation or strain. Although they may have questioned our diaconal involvement, these people never allowed anything to interfere with our relationships. Among this group, support and encouragement for our efforts abounded. What a joy these friends have been!

In addition to those who had been a part of our lives for some time, as a direct result of our diaconal commitment, Phil and I now found ourselves involved with three new groups of people—those to whom we ministered, those with whom we ministered because of Phil's ordination, and those in the diaconate. Even though it was a sharing of our Catholic faith which had brought us together, once again, we were both a part of and apart from each community.

Although Phil's ministry took him to many churches throughout the diocese, he did most of his work at our Holy Family parish where the average parishioner who was not involved in Church programs had not been aware that Phil was studying for the diaconate until he was installed as a candidate. With time, his involvement had become more and more evident as he had functioned first as a lector and then as a Eucharistic minister. Three months before Phil's ordination, an article explaining the diaconate and our family's involvement had appeared in our parish newsletter. However, it was not until after ordination that parishioners first saw my husband in his role as a deacon.

An understandable confusion caused many people some concern. "Phil is either an electrician or a deacon. He can't be both." "Why ordain a *married* man in the first place? Especially one with a large family!" "What do we call him?" "Can he hear confessions?" "Will he tell his wife what I say?" Fortunately, with time, came an increased understanding as well as an acceptance, an appreciation, and an admiration for my husband and his efforts by what seemed to be the majority of parishioners.

Our faith made us one with the people of our parish. The Philip Mraz family remained registered at the rectory office with the other families; our children attended the parish grade school; and we were still included in the mailing of the offertory envelopes. But our diaconal experience and lifetime commitment made us different from all the others, even those involved in ministry.

Among those on our parish staff, there was no one like us. The lay persons had not made a lifetime commitment, and the clergy and religious did not have a spouse and a family to complicate their lives. Yet we were still a part of each of these groups.

Happily, from the time we had become a part of the diaconate, all five bishops and many priests had welcomed us and had shown their support and acceptance by attending various diaconate events. Throughout the diocese, most of those involved in ministry with Phil were very accepting of him and his work as well as of me and my supportive role. "I'm glad for our deacon's help," one priest told me and then added with a smile, "As a matter of fact, he can take over as much of my work as he wants!" However, knowing that these feelings were not shared by all, I did some more probing.

"You're right," I was told. "Personally, I feel each one of us ought to be able to celebrate our own gift with dignity and be able to function fully in our individual roles. Although the diaconate and the priesthood appear similar, they are different. Deacons have their job; I have mine. Many priests and religious accept deacons fully and are not at all threatened by their presence. There are others who are not as enthusiastic about the diaconate, but are very accepting. Then, there are those who think of deacons as second-class citizens with very limited training or who are not accepting at all. Some even feel threatened by a deacon's presence as though deacons were in competition with them."

From a statement one priest made, there seemed to be some envy, too. "You have the best of both worlds," he had told one deacon. "Maybe so," the deacon had replied, "but if that is true, then it must also be true that I have the worst of both worlds."

I suppose some concern, curiosity, nonacceptance, and

resentment was only natural, but what I had not expected was that many of the most insensitive and hurtful things that were happening to the deacons and their wives were coming from the deacons' fellow clergy, the priests.

"As the deacon's wife, I think I was more upset by their insensitivity than my husband," one wife said. "When my husband was no longer invited to staff meetings and confirmation dinners at our own parish, I would have liked to have confronted the priests with 'What is going on here?' When a visiting priest refused to allow my husband to assist him at our home parish—at the very altar at which my husband had been assigned to assist—I felt like parading in front of the church with a sign saying 'This priest unfair to a fellow clergyman.' However, storming the rectory or picketing in front of the church would only have caused additional problems. Although upset with the fact that my gentle, peacemaker husband was sometimes being denied his rights as a deacon, I knew that he had to make his own way and handle the hurts himself."

When such incidents occurred, the deacon was hurting and he needed his loving wife and diaconate cheerleader in a way he never had before.

Because the insensitivity of the deacons themselves has caused problems, too, it would be unfair to say that others were to blame for all of the hurt inflicted by clergy as our diocese struggled with adjusting to the diaconate. Happily, the stories of incidents that could be classified "unfair" were not nearly as abundant as those telling of overwhelming clergy support, encouragement, and acceptance—all of which were essential to effective diaconal ministry.

When wondering who was responsible for building friendly relationships among the clergy, all I had to do was remember that as the deacon's wife, I was partially in charge of helping to build them. That meant my being especially sensitive to the feelings and the needs of the priests in our diocese. This was one reason I was careful not to be too friendly with my husband, not even holding hands, when

Phil wore his Roman collar. On those occasions my spouse looked like a priest, and the clergy, religious, and laity who did not know us might think I was being overly affectionate with a priest.

My desire to help build friendly relationships among the diocesan clergy was also the reason why I was careful to protect the times when the men gathered together as an all-male group. Only once was I invited to accompany Phil when his ministry outside our parish included a dinner invitation, and then I did not go. That did not mean that I did not want to accompany or felt uneasy about accompanying my husband. However, it sounded as though I was the only woman invited, and I preferred to wait for an invitation to an event that would include other women. When Phil went alone, he had time to come to know some of his fellow clergy, and the priests attending could get to know a little more about the diaconate without feeling threatened by my presence.

When asked what they saw as the role of the deacon's wife, most of the priests interviewed told me they felt the deacon's ministry was his wife's ministry, too. Although their thinking was correct, many of them apparently failed to understand that some of the wives in the program can only be at their husband's side by being their deacon's quiet, almost invisible support at home.

When I asked how the deacon's wife fit into the structure of the Church, one priest told me he thought she resembled an appendix. "You are there because of Phil," he told me. "But you must feel useless."

In a way, "appendix" was an appropriate term, for if Phil had not been ordained, I certainly would not have attended so many Church functions. But a more apt description would have been that I was with Phil, not because I had tagged along, but because I was one with him.

Overall, in word and action my husband and I attempted to show that Phil was clergy and that we were both willing to work with, support, and encourage others involved in ministry. Furthermore, we could expect no more of those with whom we worked than to have them support us to the extent they were able. There was a special beauty and joy to be found in our friendships with the clergy, religious, and committed laity. Phil and I were together in a community of people committed to active ministry—a community that was by far more supportive and encouraging than nonaccepting.

As for the relationships in our life that were not what we would have liked, we had just as much responsibility to do what we could to improve them as the other persons involved. The responsibility for continuously building a relationship with another person rests on both parties. It would have been unrealistic to expect to be pathfinders in this reinstated vocation without experiencing some rejection. There will probably always be some people who will not approve of a married man taking on the role of clergy.

Fortunately, there was one community of clergy who understood and fully accepted Phil as a man ordained to be a helpmate to bishops, priests, and parish staffs—a man who, at the same time, had a unique ministry of his own. This group recognized the importance of the role of the deacon's wife and could relate to what we were experiencing in a very real way. Here was a community of which we were definitely a part. It was, of course, the diaconate community.

The other deacons and their families had been through the program's application process, too. They had experienced firsthand the challenge of the rigorous time in formation. They had also struggled to find answers to some important questions. "Is the diaconate good for me and my family?" "Is this just an ego trip, or am I really called?" Eventually, they, too, had found it necessary to come to terms with life after ordination.

A busy family schedule, however, often stood in the way of our attending the monthly diaconate meetings where Phil and I would have had at least a little time with those in the program. Not being a part of the supportive, encouraging community that had developed during formation created a void in our lives. The need for a deep sharing of faith with others prompted us to begin to attend diaconate events whenever possible and to schedule group get-togethers for a social time and a sharing of ideas and prayer. From the first, praying together and sharing our faith helped to give each of us a spiritual uplift which was not available anywhere else. This was invaluable, especially when we were spiritually drained.

At first, even with this group, there was not an open sharing of our struggles. Then comments like "I'm so busy that I have no time to pray" and "There are not enough hours in the day to do all I want to do" eventually began to creep into the conversation. Here were some feelings I could relate to! And here was one place I could tell it like it was without hurting Phil or his ministry.

In talking with the other wives, I learned some of them had used my painful ". . . you might as well move into the rectory!" line too. Knowing without a doubt that what we were feeling as deacons' wives was being felt by others gave us the strength and courage to work through our diaconate feelings each in our own way and in our own time.

Listening and sharing, we deacons and wives began to find answers as we learned from and with each other. Once shared, our struggles and concerns became less of a burden. It was refreshing, almost a relief, to find others who understood us and our complicated new life-style—others who could help us to grow. However, the talk at these gatherings was not entirely of a serious nature.

"I offered to drive the bishop who had a torn ligament in his leg to a confirmation in the next county. On the way my car got a flat tire and I had no spare. There we were standing along the highway, the bishop on crutches and both of us in Roman collars thumbing a ride. We arrived at our destination in a pickup truck. The bishop had ridden up front with the driver while I had ridden outside in the cargo area of the truck," one deacon related.

"As Mass was ending, I became flustered and I couldn't remember whether to say 'Lord' or 'God,' so I said, 'Go in peace to love and serve the *Gord*,'" another said.

In sharing funny stories and embarrassing moments, we were able to laugh and take life a little less seriously. Moreover, in sharing our lives and our faith, those of us in the community became family for each other. Nowhere else could we find this type of closeness.

One important lesson that our diaconal involvement had taught me was that I needed others to understand me and to help me to grow. The diaconate—the people within it and the program itself—had helped me in so many ways. Here, I was encouraged to come to know and accept myself and to feel a sense of accomplishment not simply as a deacon's wife but as a woman as well. Here was one community in which I was comfortable being myself—totally, completely myself. Here I was able to share myself and my faith as fully as I wished, knowing that I would be both understood and accepted. No other community was able to meet my needs in these areas in the same faith-filled way. Yet even here there were differences—personalities, family sizes and lifestyles, our parishes with their varying sizes and staffs, and the individuality of each man's ministry with its own set of joys and frustrations.

There could be no doubt; Phil and I were a part of and at the same time apart from many communities. It was no wonder that our relationships with God and with each other were so important. It was only when we as a married couple were truly one with the Lord that Phil and I were comfortable with being "a part of and apart from" others. Furthermore, it was only then that we were comfortable answering the call to ministry which we had received—a call to minister to the People of God, each in our own way, but neither of us in our wildest dreams could have imagined just what sort of unusual ministry was to come.

11

Thy Will Be Done

Three and one-half years after Phil's ordination, my father was admitted to the Cleveland Clinic for a biopsy of a small spot which had shown up on chest x-rays taken at his annual physical. The lung was cancerous.

Over the next three or four months, many thoughts made their way through my head. My father had cancer. Why? What had Dad done to deserve this? He was a lector, a commentator, an extraordinary minister of the Eucharist. Certainly a man who had been so involved in bringing Christ to others did not deserve this kind of "reward." The answer to my question "Why?" was a simple "Why not?" What made me think that cancer should only strike the "bad guys"? Perhaps I could convince the Lord that my father still had a lot of untapped potential and that, if healed, my dad could continue to do much to serve his heavenly Father.

My father's illness brought home to me my own humanness. I, too, was terminal; it would merely be a matter of time before I would die also. Facing the fragility of my own existence for the first time in my life caused considerable soul-searching about the meaning of life.

With time, the pain and frustration subsided, and I stopped trying to bargain for my father's healing. The reality was that my father was living with lung cancer—lung cancer which in all probability would someday take his life. Finally, with an inner peace and acceptance, I began to do everything I could to make the best of a very difficult situation.

While learning to cope with my father's illness and eventual death, there was something at home which was beginning to cause me concern, too. Even before my father's surgery, Phil had begun to complain that his stomach did not feel right, and his uncomfortable feeling had lasted well over a month. What with my father's illness, Phil's being laid off from work again, and our little Andy's upcoming surgery to remove his oversized tonsils, there had been so much to worry about that I was fairly confident Phil's stomach problem was just the result of stress.

"Everything is fine. It's just nerves and the doctor suggested I slow down," Phil told me after a visit to his internist.

But his discomfort persisted. A complete series of upper and lower gastrointestinal x-rays offered no further clues—only confirmation of a clean bill of health. Despite the fact that Phil had slowed down his life-style and was taking medicines designed to relax his stomach, his discomfort continued to increase along with a rapidly developing middle-aged abdominal bulge. My concern for Phil had grown right along with his physical discomfort and his trouser size. Feeling there was no more he could do, our internist referred Phil to a stomach specialist.

"The specialist wants me in the hospital right away," my husband told me when he came home after his appointment. "Apparently he thinks something is wrong."

From there things moved rapidly along. Phil's one week hospital stay included many tests, a biopsy of a small suspicious spot on his colon, and the verdict—CANCER of the colon. By the time it was discovered, the diseased cells had already spread and were seeding the inside of Phil's abdominal cavity. Surgery would only weaken him; chemotherapy was our only medical hope to control the disease. Phil was too young for this type of cancer. He had exhibited none of the usual symptoms. Colon cancer runs in families, but no close relative had had it. "An extremely rare, extremely unusual case of cancer," we were told. However, the words "extremely rare" and "extremely unusual" were little consolation.

Although I had not considered cancer a possible cause of the discomfort Phil was feeling, I had come to suspect that something was very wrong. This time when I heard the word CANCER, I did not get angry or question. After the original shock had worn off and I had had a good cry, I found myself simply accepting Phil's colon cancer as a part of God's plan for us, and I began asking the Lord what he wanted us to do with this illness.

Along with the diagnosis of Phil's cancer, our life became busier than ever before which made my role as team manager that much more difficult. Some days there were no telephone calls or visitors. Other days there were ten or more calls and several visitors. Here, my role as my deacon's protector was taking on a new dimension. There were times when Phil was not up to seeing anyone. Sometimes when people telephoned to see if they could stop in, I would tell them "Not today" because that was what was best for Phil.

In addition to making sure things were as normal and peaceful as possible at home, as head cheerleader in charge of keeping Phil's spirits lifted, I was determined to make sure my husband did not spend his days sitting around feeling sorry for himself.

Because working toward goals had been good for us in the past, we realized from the first that we needed something to look forward to and to keep focused on during our fight against Phil's illness. Diaconal ministry seemed to be the best thing to keep my deacon husband and me going.

"No matter what the results of your tests are," I had remarked to Phil the night before he was told he had cancer, "and no matter what you feel like, we can still minister to others. If we are not able to minister in any other way, we can always minister by our example." Once uttered, I put the thought out of my head.

Phil tried returning to work as an electrician, but he was not capable of doing heavy physical labor. Yet there was no reason why he could not continue doing the same works for the Church which he had been able to accomplish before his cancer had been diagnosed. Ministry's basic requirements began with mental preparation—getting programs or homilies together. A limited amount of physical exertion was called for in carrying out the programs, assisting at Mass, leading a prayer service, or baptizing a baby. So Phil's ministry as an ordained deacon continued—cancer and all. Timed in order not to overtax him, these activities were indeed an impetus to keep him going and a valuable means of keeping his spirits lifted.

Meanwhile, my role as health counselor had greatly expanded. We worked hard to fight Phil's cancer. Dr. Jim Cunningham, the oncologist in charge of the chemotherapy, tried everything possible to rid Phil's body of the dreaded disease. At first it seemed that the treatment was helping, and after six months Dr. Cunningham told us he felt Phil's condition had stabilized. However, I was not happy with the slight changes I had noticed in Phil's condition. I had a sick inner feeling that things were not as good as they seemed.

Ten months after Phil's cancer had been diagnosed we began to see a steady decline in his physical condition. Then, books on healing through prayer and on holistic medicine and visits to a doctor of preventive medicine opened up other possible avenues for Phil's healing.

If he would not receive a physical healing, then I needed to know that we had done absolutely everything we could, that we had explored every possible avenue of healing. Of course, God would heal Phil in all the ways in which he needed to be healed no matter what we did. But just sitting around waiting for the Lord to do all the work did not seem right.

From the first we had begun to pray diligently for Phil's physical healing, and in pursuit of that end, I had made inquiries about Fr. Ralph DiOrio's healing ministry. These led to our joining a bus trip to Worcester, Massachusetts, where we experienced the first of many charismatic healing services. Meanwhile, we prayed daily at home. Each evening some of the children and I prayed with Phil and anointed him with blessed oil from a nearby shrine. In addition, Phil and I began to attend our parish prayer group's weekly meetings more regularly; when it became increasingly difficult for Phil to leave the house, one or two members of the prayer group came to our home almost nightly to pray with us.

Prayer coupled with ministry was keeping us going. My husband's diaconal ministry had continued to be productive through the first months of his illness but was gradually diminishing. After baptizing the babies of two friends, a full year after his cancer had been diagnosed, Phil remarked, "I don't think I'll be able to go to Mass anymore. In fact, at one point in the celebration, I was afraid I might collapse right at the foot of our parish altar."

With our pastor's blessing I took on a new role and became an extraordinary minister of the Eucharist bringing Communion to Phil daily. Our faith had provided our phenomenal strength all along. Above all else, prayer was the most important ingredient in each day, and looking back, I would say that personal growth seemed to be the most important product of our struggle. As the cancer had been spreading and taking over his body, Phil and I had both been making especially great strides in our spiritual growth.

Dealing with Phil's illness had taught us much. The first lesson would probably best be entitled patience. How I had wanted to know from the very first what God had planned for us. When we attended healing services I wondered if the Lord were leading us to a healing ministry. And when we began to look into holistic healing, I wondered if someday we would be involved, *together*, in helping others to fight cancer as they lived with it in faith. Gradually, I learned to let go of some of my inquisitiveness and became content with simply concentrating on what seemed most important at the moment. Eventually, I came to trust the Lord with the inner assurance that in God's own time all would be revealed.

Perseverance was the next big lesson. Working for Phil's healing was not always easy. However, having seen God heal the deaf, the blind, and the lame at Father DiOrio's services, we knew God could do *anything*, and there was always the hope that the Lord would heal Phil's seemingly incurable cancer. Thus, we continued to pray and to work toward that healing.

The third lesson during this period of our lives was about prayer itself. When Phil's cancer had first been diagnosed, it had been difficult, sometimes impossible, to pray. Even picking up a book of prayer, old formal prayers, or eloquent modern ones had done no good. The words on the paper had been simply words with no meaning, words strung together with occasional meaningless marks of punctuation scattered here and there. When I was able to pray, supplications of "Heal Phil! Heal him, Lord!" in a demanding tone of voice gradually took on a more pleading quality. "Heal him, Lord. Please, heal him." Finally, a year later, my prayer had changed to a simple "Thy will be done." For the first time in my life, that phrase had come alive with meaning. What more could Phil or I ever want; what could ever be better than what God wanted for us?

Meanwhile, Phil's prayer had been changing, also. He, too, was praying for the Lord's will and eventually found relief from his pain not in the frequent doses of morphine—even they did not alleviate his extreme discomfort—but in "walking with Jesus." He had discovered a way to spiritually, prayerfully unite his sufferings with those of our Lord, and he found peace in that union.

The lessons derived from living with cancer included more than those in patience, perseverance, and prayer. Oftentimes, a friend or neighbor would appear at our back door with groceries, fresh produce from the garden, baked goods, or a meal ready to go. Neighbors generously watched our children while Phil and I were at the hospital. One friend even gave us a ride to the hospital at midnight when Phil had difficulty swallowing—a side effect of his chemotherapy treatment a few days before. A group of Holy Family parishioners planned a steak roast in Phil's honor, and our parish social action commission treated us to dinner-for-two at a nice restaurant nearby. God's loving care for us was being overwhelmingly manifested through his people.

"Saying 'thank you' has become a way of life!" I exclaimed to my friend Kay one day. "Prayers, food, flowers, cards, babysitting, so many generous gifts, you name it—all we seem to do is take. Phil and I do not want to take; we want to give!" In my frustration, I began to cry.

"You are giving," my friend replied calmly. "Dottie, you and Phil are giving us so much." Kay tried to comfort me with her words and a hug. "Because of Phil's illness, many have learned to appreciate their spouses, their marriages, their children, and their friends so much more. They have also learned to value each day of their lives. Everyone who has seen you or who knows you has learned so much. As much as I hate to say it, you and Phil are paving the way for the rest of us. You are showing by your example how to live in faith with a serious illness."

One thing was certain: living with Phil's illness was teaching me that I would never be able to live with an I'll-do-it-myself attitude again. Phil and I were beginning to realize that as independent as we had felt in the past, we were actually totally dependent upon the Lord for *all* things. God was in charge, not us. He had been in charge all along. Now we were learning to trust him completely and unquestioningly and to freely share our growth in faith with others.

"We know that God makes all things work together for the good of those who have been called according to his decree" (Rom 8:28). It was true. How could I be angry with my God who was not only showing me his love for us, but also literally pointing out some of the good that was coming to us and to others because of our own painful experience with cancer.

Hard as it seemed, I knew that our loving Father had only our best interests at heart. I was so convinced that once, when reading a book about the power of praise in prayer, I actually felt my whole being joyfully praising God for Phil's cancer. I did not praise the Lord for Phil's pain, of course; the last thing I wanted was for my husband to be hurting. But since we seemed to have no choice in the matter, I praised God for his creative use of Phil's illness and for all the wonderful things he was doing in, with, and through our suffering. Although I did not understand what I felt and knew this was not what a loving wife "should feel," the feelings were very real. But Phil was the one whose body the cancer was consuming. How did he feel?

"When I saw a picture of the Sacred Heart a couple of weeks ago, I really wanted to reach out and touch that heart," Phil confided. "I don't want to upset you, but at that moment my whole being wanted to reach out and be united with the Lord."

Once the sick feeling in the pit of my stomach had passed, I experienced an immense sense of relief. I knew from Phil's words that he was ready for death—if that was the Lord's will for him.

"Thy will be done." If I truly meant that prayer, then I would need to come to terms with one more thing— the fact that the man whom I thought of as being mine was not really mine at all. He never had been. Phil was simply on loan to me from the Lord to whom he really belonged. *My* deacon? No. *God's* deacon. At Phil's ordination I had sensed that I was giving up a small part of my claim to my husband. In living our busy diaconate life-style, I had been called upon to give up an even larger share of it. Now, if the Lord really was calling Phil home, I had no right to try to hold on to any of that claim. It was time for me to let go; in spite of the fact that I was not about to give up hope for Phil's physical healing until he breathed his last, I could see that the Lord was drawing my husband ever closer to himself.

"I just want to die," Phil told me one August night. Living with cancer had been a way of life for us for thirteen months, and my husband had finally reached the point where he was tired of fighting what appeared to be a losing battle. He was tired of handling the pain. Deacon Phil Mraz was ready to go home.

One morning three weeks later, Phil's breakfast would not stay in his stomach. Breakfast had been the only meal which had been staying down for several days, but this morning, it wanted no part of him. "I think you had better take me to the hospital," my husband told me.

"Let me take a shower first," I pleaded. "I need to set a load of wash, too." I was procrastinating and I knew it. Obviously Phil's colon was blocked. We had been warned of this possibility when his cancer had been diagnosed. At that time, we had been told the solution was simple—a colostomy. Then, they had told us, my husband would be able to come home. But why, if that was the case, was I stalling for time? All of a sudden the reason for my procrastination became clear. I started to cry. "If I take you," I sobbed to Phil, "I'm afraid I'll never bring you home."

Phil was sitting in the same comfortable high-backed rocker I had been relaxing in, pregnant, when he had first told me about the diaconate. Now he pulled me to himself and held me in his arms. "No, Honey. The doctors will do what they can, and then I'll be home."

Thus, Phil and I proceeded to the final step of our journey with cancer. "Your husband is in too weakened a condition for surgery. No surgeon would dare operate," the doctor told me. "All we can do is keep him comfortable."

"I want to go home," Phil told me. Oh, how I wanted him home, too! So began the process of convincing the doctors that this was something we both wanted and then of making the necessary arrangements for ambulance, hospital bed, water-bed mattress, and hospice nurses.

The day before Phil was to come home, I settled in for the allotted visiting hours while trying to keep my husband's spirits lifted. By 3:00 the next afternoon Phil would be home! Even knowing that caring for him would not be easy, I could hardly wait to have him back where he belonged, where he could be with our children.

About 8:00 that evening, Phil very calmly told me, "I don't think I'll make it through the night."

"Do you want me to stay?" I asked.

"Yes," he answered.

"Are you scared?"

"No."

"Neither am I," I replied. It was true; there was a surprising peace within me.

In light of Phil's comment, I was beginning to wonder whether or not he would actually make it home the next day. Not wishing to take a chance on Phil's dying without seeing his offspring at least one more time, I arranged for all five children to come to the hospital about 9:30 that night. In turn, they each had their own private time to say "I love you" and "God bless you and keep you safe." In addition, their father had a special message for each one of them.

Then, for the last time, we all gathered together around Phil's bed—a whole family united. This time it was not the family deacon but the deacon's wife who led a very short, very simple prayer service.

Our eldest son Philip, now age sixteen, asked to remain with me at the hospital. The others went home.

Phil was awake off and on for the next few hours. He

wanted to talk to us, but his jaw was not cooperating, and as a result, his enunciation was poor.

"Ahh wuv ouu!" Phil repeated over and over with force in a determined attempt to make us understand. "Ahh wuv ouu!"

I had absolutely no idea what he was trying to tell me. "It's okay, just rest now. I love you," I told him.

Phil settled into a peaceful sleep soon after. An hour later I heard a rattle in his chest. His lungs were filling with fluid. Standing at his bedside, I simply told my deacon husband over and over again, "I love you, I love you, I love you." It was the same message he had tried so hard to make me understand only a little while before. My trembling fingers stroked my beloved's forehead and face. "I love you, I love you, I love you . . ." Phil heard as his spirit passed from this world to the next.

Deacon Philip J. Mraz had gone home to his heavenly Father, and for Phil, Bishop Hickey's admonition to the men at ordination had now been fulfilled completely.

"My brothers, be always men of deep faith, of constant hope, of burning love—deacons of the Church of Cleveland. And then, when you meet the Lord on the last day, you shall hear from him those blessed words, 'Well done my good and faithful servant. Enter into the joy of your Lord.'"

12

The Deacon's Widow

It was finished. In a few seconds Phil's lungs had ceased to breathe, his heart had stopped beating, and his spirit had moved on to a better world. In the same few seconds, I had ceased to be the deacon's wife. I was now the deacon's widow—the first in the diocese of Cleveland.

When we were escorted to the hospital's night exit, my son Philip and I were carrying Phil's things, and in the crook of her arm, the head nurse on duty carried a thick medical file now sealed shut. The file was Phil's. The finality was beginning to sink in. My heart felt the pain of something important left behind. It was Phil. He would never again be going home with me. I felt empty and awkward—as though I were leaving a part of myself behind.

Deacon Phil Mraz may have entered into the joy of his reward, but as his widow, I was left with plenty to do. With much help the arrangements for his funeral were completed rather quickly, and all was ready for the wake to be held in Holy Family Church on the Thursday and Friday before Labor Day.

Phil's casket had been placed in front of the right side altar. Over his secular clothes my husband was wearing his long white ordination alb and the stole which I had designed and painstakingly appliquéd with grapes and wheat as my ordination gift to him. Around his neck was a narrow strip of rawhide from which hung a three-inch wooden cross, the cross Phil had worn when ministering to the People of God. In the corner of the casket was the beloved lectionary which he had used so often in prayer and ministry. Those who came would find a peacefulness about Phil's body, but many would also notice something unusual about it.

There was a beautiful, smooth, almost translucent quality about Phil's hands as he lay in state. Even the embalmer had remarked that although Phil's whole body had been racked by cancer, his hands were perfect. A deacon's hands are special hands. They are the hands that are about the Lord's work—in all aspects of life. Phil's hands were the ones that had held me, played games with the children, and done work around the house in his role as husband and father. They were the hands that had pulled wire and hung fixtures in his work as an electrician. And they were the hands that had baptized a baby, blessed a bride and groom, distributed Holy Communion, and held the hands of others in prayer in his ministry as a deacon. A deacon's hands are blessed hands with a special mission—a mission of love to family, job, and diaconal ministry.

Both evenings, the visitation hours began with a short prayer service conducted by deacons whom Phil had helped to vest at their ordinations. So many people came to pay their respects. It was as though all of the love and concern which had been shown us throughout our lives, but most especially during Phil's illness, had been wrapped up in one big package presented to me and the children over those two days.

"I do not believe it," one of Phil's brothers remarked as he shook his head and wiped away his tears. "I did not even know my own brother." Perhaps the eyes of many were being opened now in a far better way than they would have been had Phil and I tried to explain to family and friends what our faith commitment was and what it meant.

Phil's funeral Mass was scheduled for 12:30 on Saturday afternoon. Before leaving for the church that day, there were emotions welling up within me which were strangely familiar. Of course! Joy was what I had felt on our wedding day seventeen years before. Come to think of it, the excitement within me was much like that which I had experienced on Phil's ordination day. Although I knew overwhelming, triumphal joy was not what a widow should feel, even as the children and I followed my husband's closed casket down the center aisle, the feeling remained.

When we reached the front of Holy Family Church, I followed my children as they filed into the front pew on the right-hand side—the very pew which our family had been assigned a little more than five years before when Phil and his classmates had been ordained.

Phil's casket was in the aisle next to me, precisely where he had stood when he had stated his words of commitment at ordination. "I am ready and willing," he had said. But this time, he would not speak those words, nor would he return to the pew to stand at my side. This time I would stand alone.

Phil's funeral celebration, which he carefully planned during the last weeks of his life, included time for tears, laughter, and applause. Rather than the usual funeral atmosphere, there was a feeling of a very special, very holy celebration taking place—a celebration of a life well lived.

"I feel so good. I do not understand it, but I do," Phil's brother who had been crying the night before told me after the Mass. Even I, who had been so much a part of Phil's life and his death, did not fully understand, but I, too, felt good.

Being a realist, I knew that eventually I would undoubtedly experience all of the feelings and emotions which a widow generally has. Yet, I had the feeling that my experience of sharing in Phil's lifetime commitment would make my grief different in some way—possibly add another dimension to it. And that is what it did.

Although my husband was no longer physically present, just as our wedding and his ordination had added marriage and diaconal ministry to my life, Phil's death and his funeral added something very special, too. What took place within my spirit at the time of that celebration was something more than the simple renewal of the promises I had made at Phil's ordination. There I had processed with Phil and, along with five other wives, I had stood before our bishop. The verbal "I do" I stated on that day had signified my personal commitment to a new way of life filled with quiet, supportive ministry to Phil and to the People of God.

When the children and I followed Phil's casket up the aisle at my husband's funeral, I once again processed toward a new commitment. This time, however, rather than standing before my bishop to do so, I had once again pledged myself to a life of service when I followed Phil's casket, when I assumed my place in the front pew, and when I stood at the lectern to deliver a Communion reflection.

At Phil's funeral, my "I do" had been expressed in actions rather than in words. It had been a nonverbal consent given by my whole being which had committed all of me to a new way of life where once again I felt drawn to a ministry to the People of God. But this time, my commitment had not hinged on that of my husband, for the ministry of service to which I had now promised myself was to be mine and God's alone.

Barb, a deacon's wife more recently widowed when her husband Art died suddenly of a heart attack, told me, "At the time of Art's death, I felt a strong need to let our bishop and the director of the diaconate program know I am available to help them in any way. But I also felt called upon to reaffirm my commitment to the diaconate and to the ministry Art and I shared. Because I am not ordained, there is much that I can not do, but I do feel I have an obligation to be involved in the commitments we shared. I have cho-

sen to reaffirm my commitment to ministry largely because
of the diaconal commitment and experience I shared with
Art." Perhaps these are normal feelings for the deacon's
widow.

In any case I believe the uplifting, joyful feeling at the
time of Phil's death had been most appropriate, for it had
all been a part of my becoming a bride of the Church. That
fact would explain why for the first few months following
Phil's death I felt as though I was once again on a honeymoon. This time, my honeymoon was enhanced by the
kindness and caring of many people. So much was happening in my life that, even though I missed my husband
tremendously as only a widowed person could fully understand, I was surprised to find I awoke eager to meet each
new day. In spite of the pain, life was good.

Of course, the honeymoon did not last. Those first busy
days were soon followed by other quieter ones when I had
time to accomplish the various necessary tasks required of
a widow. Eventually, there was time to reflect upon all that
had happened as well as to think about the future.

The first and most obvious change in my life was that
Phil was no longer physically present; I was no longer a
wife. For more than seventeen years, my life had revolved
around my husband. Our children and my own outside interests had been good for me, but Phil, his activities, and
his needs had always been the center of my life. How could
I not miss so many things?—preparing his favorite meals,
the look on his face and the shake of his head as he affectionately remarked, "You are something else!" the quiet
times when we were simply alone together, the laughter
and shouts of joy as he played with the children, the times
when we were with our family and friends, and the times
when I participated in or simply supported his ministry.
All of these were beautiful memories, but they were just
that—memories, bringing a mixture of joy and pain.

In my heart I knew I would mourn my beloved husband's death for the rest of my days. Actually, I would not

be grieving simply over my loss of Phil but also over the part of myself that had died with him. Because Phil and I had been one in so many ways, I was missing a substantial part of myself.

Accepting the reality of being a widow would mean fully admitting the disheartening fact that Phil, my old reason for living, needed to be replaced with a whole list of new reasons—none of which, in my estimation, were quite as good as the old one. Then too, there was the emptiness, the loneliness, the change in the family finances, a new independence, and the loss of Phil's diaconal ministry, along with a whole series of other easily recognized drawbacks of widowhood. Just as I had once been disillusioned with my marriage and with the diaconate, I now found myself disillusioned with my role as a deacon's widow. Knowing from past experience that I did not enjoy hurting, I was determined to spend as little time as possible adjusting to this new state of life. Feeling sure that God wanted me to be able to live comfortably with being the deacon's widow, I began to pray for the graces and the strength to do just that.

Unconditionally accepting widowhood as God's will brought an inner peace. That combined with a joy in being a mother and ministering to others, along with a sense of anticipation as I looked to the future, allowed me to become increasingly more contented with what I had once felt would always be a rather awkward state.

Oddly enough, here too in my third "marriage," the same stages seem to be cycling. From honeymoon through contentment, but always within the final stage of contentment, my life is ever changing, just as it had been before. As a widow who has committed her life to the Lord, I know my life and the lives of my children will never again be the same as they were when Phil was alive. But life has settled down to what I call our "new normal," and it is a normal of which I am determined to make the best.

Life continues to be busy. "Family first, then work, and finally ministry." The old rule of thumb which I learned in the diaconate is just as important to me now as it was when Phil was alive. My many-faceted motherhood begins in loving and supporting my children in all things. It continues through nearly the entire list of responsibilities I once had as Deacon Phil's wife only now I fulfill most of those roles as mother while trying to keep our family united in work, in play, and in prayer. It culminates in giving my children their freedom, thereby, I hope, enabling them to become all God is calling them to be. In so doing, I am attempting to raise them in such a manner that my children will grow secure in my love and in the knowledge that they are of the utmost importance to me.

As the deacon's widow, one of my primary concerns for my children is that they continue to have as normal a childhood as possible. Where the diaconate itself had once posed a threat to our offspring's well-being, that threat has now been compounded by the fact that their deacon dad has died, and they have a mother who remains very committed to her faith.

While my husband is no longer here to help keep our family faith-centered, the memory of his faith-filled life remains a legacy for us all. Sharing our faith is now especially important because it is our faith which ultimately keeps us growing and draws the many aspects of our family's life together. I can not claim that we have it "all together." However, just as the diaconate had once drawn our family closer, our faith combined with the experience of Phil's death has drawn the children and me closer than ever. Here we are, six people facing life united as a somewhat different family unit. As a matter of fact, I still see our family as being radically different and each family member as being transformed daily. That, of course, has created another problem.

Just as we had been after Phil's ordination, the children and I continue to be a part of and, at the same time, apart from those in all of the communities in our lives. For me, especially, the fact that I am a widow seems to have widened the gap because few among our close family and friends are widowed, and those who are have not experienced the diaconate. In addition, many of the old barriers remain. Others' increased concerns for our family's well-being, my busy, draining schedule, the addition of more new friends, a continued resentment or awe on the part of some, the expanded experiences provided by the diaconate program, my continued growth in faith, and the inability to share all of myself with most, but not all, of the others in my life— so many things still contribute to my feeling apart in many situations.

Other than our diaconal faith experiences, perhaps there is less separating our family now from those to whom and with whom we ministered than when Phil was alive since we no longer have a clergyman living in our home. Because I feel more deeply wedded to my faith than ever before, I still consider myself a part of the group of those with a lifetime commitment to ministry. However, in spite of my personal commitment, I could not blame the majority of the clergy and religious for viewing me as less a part of them than I was when Phil was alive—not even as an appendix. The majority of clergy and religious would most likely think me less a part of them, that is, except for those within the diaconate.

At the time of Phil's death, I had immediately assumed that without a deacon husband, I would no longer have a place within or, for the matter, a need for the diaconate community. But I was wrong.

"*We* need *you*," one of the deacon's wives told me at Phil's wake.

"Need me? How could they?" I wondered. After all, Phil was the deacon, not I. But what I was forgetting was the fact that each one of us is a gift to all of the others, and everyone is needed in order to make the diaconate community whole. The fact that others feel I still belong is obvious. I continue to receive the diaconal mailings, am greeted warmly whenever I attend diaconate functions or continuing-education classes, and now have my name listed with the others on the community roster under "Wives of Deceased Deacons."

At first, though others felt I belonged, I was not certain I would be able to handle the emotional aspect of being with the community. The opening song of the first special ceremony I attended brought tears to my eyes. It was one Phil had chosen for his funeral and was a reminder that in some unexplainable way my husband, too, would always be a part of our diaconate community.

Actually, being present for special liturgies or other diaconate events is not as hard as I was once afraid it might be. Although there are times when I see a deacon assisting at the altar or hear of his ministry that I long to have all of that back, surprisingly enough, those occasions are rare. When they do occur, a quick reminder that Phil's work is done brings me back to the reality that mine is not, and it will never be the same. What I feel most often is pride in the deacons of our diocese and in the service to which they are dedicated. Therefore, my ministry of support and affirmation for the diaconate is just as important to me now as it was when my husband was alive.

In order for that ministry to be effective, it is essential that I know the people in the ever-expanding community as well as what is happening in the program. Each time I am with those in the diaconate is like a joyful homecoming for me. Here are people who truly understand my commitment to ministry because they, too, have made a similar promise. Here are friends who are very much family to me—friends who allow me to share myself completely and who accept me as I am. How could I ever have thought I could divorce myself from the diaconate? With the possible exception of several close family members and friends, no others are able to provide me with the kind of support and encouragement I continue to receive from this group. Despite Phil's death, this is one place where I still belong. The diaconate is just as much a part of me as I am of it.

At the time of Phil's death, I had felt an unexpected sense of relief in knowing that no matter what I would do from then on, it could no longer affect my husband or his ministry in any way. In spite of my new sense of freedom, I remain in a delicate position in my parish and in my community, for my actions continue to reflect not only upon me and my family but also upon my Church and upon the diaconate program as well. As the deacon's widow, I find a new desire to protect the diaconate, and its image has replaced my old desire to protect Phil and his ministry.

Two very familiar, practical helps have permitted me to live peacefully with the changes which have transpired in every area of my life since Phil's death—communication and ordering my priorities. Communication begins with the Lord and with a few close friends who are willing to listen in confidence whenever I need to talk and who are unquestioningly accepting of me and my sometimes unusual innermost thoughts and feelings. Our relationships are encouraging, supportive, and comfortable, in much the same way as my relationship with Phil had been. More importantly, these open and honest friendships are essential for my personal well-being as well as for keeping my life in proper order.

Experience has taught me that my relationship with the Lord must be first on my list of priorities, for it forms the basis of my existence and holds the many facets of my life together. Although in the eyes of the world I am becoming more and more independent, with the lessons in patience, perseverance, and prayer learned during Phil's illness, I am developing an ever-deepening trust in and dependence upon my heavenly Father. An increased realization of and appreciation for God's Presence has sparked an unquenchable spiritual hunger within me. Once again, the diaconate program has not left me completely on my own for my spiritual growth. The various ceremonies continue to give me the opportunities I need to recommit myself to doing the Lord's will. These rituals, the days of recollection for the wives, and the annual diaconate retreat still provide spiritual food which is unavailable anywhere else.

Taking care of my spiritual health is important in itself, but it is only one aspect of seeing to my total well-being. My physical, social, emotional, and intellectual health remain essential in order for me to successfully accept the challenge of life as a deacon's widow as well as meet the needs of others.

Seeing to my emotional well-being is probably the most challenging of all. How fortunate it is that in adjusting to our commitment to ministry, I realized the importance of maintaining my individuality. If, as the deacon's wife, I had tried to hide behind my husband's long white alb, wherever would I get my self-identity now when, as the deacon's widow, there is no longer an alb to hide behind? The temptation to hide behind others still exists. As a single parent of five, it would be easy for me to become a full-time parent with my life centered solely on my children and their interests. But activities which I find self-fulfilling and which allow me to continue to discover my unique gifts and talents provide me pleasure as well as assure me that I am truly a woman in my own right, a woman capable of making my own contribution to the universe—deacon husband or not.

When my relationship with God and taking care of myself head my priority list, I have found that neither is that time-consuming, but that both are essential in freeing me to concentrate my efforts and energies on my children, my household duties, and our outside activities, including ministry—in that order. I am trying to set realistic goals and to live each day fully while attempting to concentrate on accomplishing whatever seems most important at the moment. By having my life fairly well ordered, I am able to achieve some semblance of a delicate balance in my life and a sense of peace within.

Inner peace was especially important for me immediately following Phil's death because, at first, I was required to give up even more of my privacy than I had been called upon to relinquish when Phil was alive. Fortunately, I have come a long way in accepting myself as I am with no pretenses—no play acting, no putting on airs—just a very human imperfect me with a willingness to work on correcting my faults. This has allowed me increased freedom to be myself, which is fortunate because, with widowhood, the struggle to stand up to others who try to tell me who I should be or how I should act or feel has intensified. Ultimately, I alone am responsible to the Lord for myself and all of my actions.

"Who is Dottie?" remains a question not yet answered in its entirety. What that has meant all along is that I am a woman forever emerging. I am a woman who hopes to continue growing until I die, even though growth often means accepting the numerous and sometimes painful challenges of life head-on. That much growth has already taken place is clearly evidenced by the fact that I have been able to peacefully accept and to help my children accept Phil's death and the more recent death of my father.

Although friends continue to say, "You haven't changed," I know that is not true. As Deacon Phil's widow, I am radically different from what I was before the diaconate entered my life. Furthermore, because of my sharing in Phil's ordination, I continue to be transformed daily. I am not the same woman today that I was before either the diaconate or Phil's death.

Through all, the one thing which remains constant is my commitment to my faith evidenced by an overwhelming desire to do the will of the Lord; somehow, I suspect that my sense of personal pride and self-worth will continue to be deeply rooted in answering my call from God to the best of my ability every day of my life. Woman, Phil's wife, mother of five, deacon's wife, then widow—the call to ministry is forever surprising me with the direction it takes.

13

Ministry

"Why put the chapters dealing with ministry at the end of this book when the main thrust of the diaconate is ministry and especially when the deacon involved in the story is no longer actively pursuing a ministry here on earth?" you might well ask. The answer is simple.

When Phil first told me of his desire to be a deacon, I assumed that ministry was doing things for others and that preaching, baptizing, directing programs, and visiting the sick were among the grand and glorious works deacons were called upon to do. At ordination I pictured my newly ordained deacon whose ministry focused on marriage and family life as one who would begin many new marriage and family programs in our parish community and bring a new zest to the Christian Family Movement. Just when, in a twenty-four-hour day, Phil was to accomplish all of these things never entered my mind. Nonetheless, I envisioned my husband as a super deacon complete with alb and stole, and I pictured him out in the world doing numerous works for the Lord.

It was not long after ordination that I became disenchanted with the fulfillment of that vision. The reality of Phil's living out his ordained commitment was not living up to my expectations because my vision of ministry had been unrealistic to begin with.

One very important ministry element that I had not considered was that ministry had to be based in prayer. At Phil's ordination, the bishop had reminded the deacons that their service to the Church would be effective only to the extent that their personal commitment to Jesus remained vital and strong. Our relationships with God—Phil's and mine, separately and together—were important for several reasons. First, all of Phil's ministry as deacon and mine as his wife flowed out of our awareness of God and his love for us. Second, in order to be faith-filled and genuine, our service had to be based in our own prayer life. Finally, the quality of our relationships with God determined the quality of our ministry, for we could not share with others what we did not have ourselves, nor could we work for the Lord if we did not take time daily to ask him for guidance and direction in that work.

In order to be *peaceful* and *effective*, however, our ministry based in prayer needed to begin in a rather surprising place—within ourselves and our own lives. It began in continuously building a loving marriage relationship, in supporting each other in all things, and in seeing to our children's needs. Ministry? Yes. It was a ministry we had been called to long before the diaconate and a ministry for which no laying on of hands was necessary.

It was true that we could minister elsewhere without meeting the needs at home, but such service in the Lord's name was never as peaceful or as effective as it could have been. I still cringe each time I recall chastizing my husband for his unusually lengthy absence one particular Sunday morning. Unfortunately, I expressed my frustration in no uncertain terms as Phil made a hasty exit to assist at Mass that morning.

"I never know how to plan anymore!" I complained. "There's almost no time for me to get to church!"

A peaceful exit for Phil? Definitely not. Nor were my husband's impromptu remarks chastizing those who arrived late for the liturgy peaceful either. Since those who most needed a reminder to be on time for Mass had undoubtedly not even arrived on the scene by the time he had spoken them, I could not in any way consider my husband's words effective ministry.

However, the incident was effective in pointing out the necessity of constantly ministering at home while we sometimes ministered elsewhere. Only when we were attempting to meet the needs of those at home was either of us able to peacefully and effectively serve others, and only then was Phil's ordained ministry worthwhile. If we were to allow *anything* to become more important than our marriage and our family, our first callings, then all of our ministry elsewhere, especially works accomplished in ministry to the marriages and families of others, would have been a farce.

Coming to understand that prayer and taking care of ourselves, each other, and our family had to come first was the first step in formulating a more reasonable definition of service in the Lord's name. But in order for my vision of ministry to be even more realistic, it was necessary to learn to deal successfully with each of the numerous ministry temptations which confronted both of us.

One of the first lures to be overcome was the desire to be *all* things to *all* people *all* of the time. Phil saw much that he would have liked to have accomplished, and many opportunities for ministry which he overlooked I saw and wanted *him* to respond to. Because we would have liked to have had the answer for each of the needs presented to us, I am convinced that, at the time of Phil's ordination, our resistance to a malady commonly referred to as the Messiah complex had been lowered. Not only had we become susceptible to the complex but we had also been infected. In extreme cases the condition is easily recognized by the rather offensive attitude of the person or persons so infected: "Here I am, world, change is on its way!" "Move over, parish staff. Here I come!"

Fortunately, the Mraz case of this malady was short-lived and manifested itself mildly in the form of frustration with not being able to answer all of the needs we saw. Here, it was necessary to remind ourselves that, as much as we might have liked, the two of us could not change the world. Whenever Phil or I tried to do too much it seemed that nothing was done well. In overcoming the temptation to perform too many of the numerous good works which I had envisioned for Phil, a rather surprising form of self-sacrifice became a part of our lives. We often had to say no to things we would have liked to have done, knowing that no was the only realistic answer for us.

Saying no to ministry requests was often difficult because from all reports most of Phil's brother deacons were involved in numerous important projects. Compared to those of the others, my husband's works sounded trivial. Phil was obviously coming in last in the subtle game of "Can You Top This?" which the men seemed to be playing when they talked with each other. Many times I was tempted to pad the list of my husband's current endeavors in order to make it sound as if he were involved in many important works, too.

Unfortunately, this was especially disconcerting because it was happening not long after ordination at precisely the time when Phil and I were struggling with the fact that we were over involved and needed to *cut back* on our outside activities. Overcoming the temptation to compete with others in the program did not prove an easy task; however, it was essential in our learning to be happy with the amount of ministry outside of our home which was appropriate for us at any given time. In the end all Phil could do was answer requests for ministry as he felt called by God rather than as others, no matter who, thought he should. When concentrating on responding in the way which was realistic and right for us, the temptation to answer to the rest of the world was no longer important.

It now seemed that my husband's good works were not going to be nearly as numerous as I had imagined. Although from time to time there had been a marked increase in his activities as indicated by the diaconate clumps on our calendar, some of Phil's other activities, like our C.F.M. small group meetings, had disappeared. My husband may have taken on more, but he had also let go of some.

Because much of Phil's ministry consisted of things he had been doing before ordination, it was time to let go of something else—my vision of Phil's performing grand and glorious works for the People of God. In its original context the word "ministry" referred to the small or humble efforts of slaves and children. I was now coming to understand ministry as meaning service in a humble form, for even Phil's more involved projects were not grandiose but simply a series of little works—endless telephone calls, letters, talks, and meetings.

In spite of the fact that service was simply small tasks done for the Lord, there was still the temptation to become puffed up with feelings of self-importance. Because often others were looking at us and at our commitment with awe, it was essential that Phil and I continually remind ourselves that his diaconal ordination had been in response to a call to be a *servant*—to serve our bishops, to work with the priests of our diocese, especially those at our parish, and to minister to the People of God. As Phil's wife, I shared in that call. We were both called to be servants to those who served; it was not a position for status but rather a lowly one. Yet there was no denying that we had received a special call to perform works on behalf of the Lord and in his name. That was something to remember, too, for the ministry was God's, not ours, and all that we accomplished was for God's honor and glory, not ours.

My vision of ministry was beginning to be more realistic; however, there were several additional temptations. To begin with, as much as we would have liked to have taken the burdens of others upon ourselves, we could not. All we could do as ministers was to walk with others while gently challenging them to change and to grow.

Looking for change and growth created two added frustrations. From experience Phil and I had discovered that change and growth are often painful. Prudent sharing of our struggles and pain was often useful in helping others to deal with their problems, but there was nothing we could do to spare others' hurt. There was also the frustration of looking for immediate results in the work we did when change and growth are usually aggravatingly slow in coming about. Here, the perseverance which the bishop had spoken of at Phil's ordination entered the picture once again.

Even though it took time for things to happen in our service to others, ministry elsewhere could definitely be more alluring and more immediately rewarding than ministry at home. Here, another temptation entered the picture. Although Phil put much time and effort into preparing a homily or a program, presenting it could be very satisfying. Once it was completed, not only did people generally tell him they appreciated his efforts, but he was also free to move on to his next ministry involvement.

That was seldom true in our home. Being with the children and me was largely thankless and was never finished. Similarly, once Phil finished a job around the house, it either needed attention again soon, or there was some other pressing task awaiting his time. As for me, my limited ministry outside the home was definitely more immediately gratifying than settling the kids' squabbles and washing clothes or dishes. The temptation was to overdo the outside involvements and enjoy the compliments or, at the very least, the satisfaction of standing back to take a look at a job well done.

When works of service seemed to be taking us away from home too often, it was time to ask "Why?" because ministry elsewhere could so easily have become an admirable form of escape from family responsibilities or unpleasant family situations. Ministry work was generally more fun than work at home, and ministry relationships were usually not as deep, as lasting, or as difficult as those in our family. Overall, service to others generally required less of us and was less draining than service at home.

Because diaconal ministry was so important to us, there was another temptation which ordained service provided. "I wish I were a full-time deacon. I could do so much more if I gave up my job and worked for the Church in ministry." We occasionally heard this longing from Phil and others. Men who had been working full-time in some ministry before ordination had automatically been involved in full-time diaconal ministry. However, one of the special aspects of the diaconate is that deacons are clergy living the life of laymen, and as such, they are a vital link between the clergy and the laity. To minister full-time would take them out of the marketplace and make them less available to most of the people they are now with every day. They would no longer be as vital a link to the everyday world. Moreover, what seems to have endeared deacons and their ministry to many people is the fact that in addition to a normal family life-style with all of its problems, deacons have the strength and the courage to commit so much of their free time to ministry *for* and *with* the People of God.

Because of Phil's diaconal ordination, he had become a member of the clergy of our diocese. He had been called to be an official shepherd looking after the Lord's flock; at the same time, my husband was one of the sheep, and so was I. Since neither of us had all of the answers, we needed to look to others within the flock for support and encouragement. How easy it was to be tempted by a false sense that ministry was giving, giving, giving, when, in reality, ministry also involves receiving.

No individual and no couple in the diaconate ministers alone. Phil's ministry, mine, and that of our family could not have been fruitful had it not been for the support of our children, our family and friends, the members of C.F.M., our parishioners, the parish staff, our pastor, the priests and bishops of our diocese, our confessors and spiritual directors, and the diaconal community—all of whom were sources of strength for us. When we were feeling drained or discouraged, their words of appreciation and encouragement helped to refresh and renew our spirits. Moreover, the gentle, understanding way they touched our lives helped our family to be faithful to the commitment we had made.

However, the most important element in the success of the ministry of a married deacon is the support and encouragement of his wife. No married deacon ministers alone. Although his wife is not ordained, she too has been called, and she shares in his ordination in an unexplainable way. Whether she is actively involved in her husband's ministry projects or simply his quiet, almost invisible support, her support is essential. That would explain why, when I was not encouraging my husband, there was tension in our relationship rather than the joy and contentment which were present when I was supporting him fully.

Of course, I was not the only spouse in our home who was called upon to be supportive. All the while Phil's ministry had been evolving, a distinct ministry uniquely my own had made its way into my life. Here, Phil's support of me and my ministry both at home and away was just as essential.

Phil and I had become one in service just as we had become one in our marriage. Ministry involved many things— listening, playing, planning and facilitating programs, praying for and with others, preparing supper for someone who was sick, officiating at weddings and wake services, and other simple things. Our two distinct ministries combined with our ministry together made a ministry unique to us as a couple; it was a ministry that was ever changing to meet our family's needs as well as the needs of those around us. Phil's ministry and mine—separate and combined, complementing and enriching each other—were one with us and we were one with them, and there was a joy in that.

It was now time to let go of one final ministry temptation—the temptation to think of Phil's diaconal ministry as his. It was not his alone. It was his, mine, ours, and our family's; it was making its own contribution to the richness of our family life and was a part of our family and an extension of it at the same time. In time we had reached the point where ministry fit peacefully into our lives. It was no longer apart from our other daily activities, separated into its own category, but rather an integral part of our daily living—a way of life for us.

At last, I had arrived at what I thought was a realistic, comprehensive definition of service in the Lord's name. "Ministry is a series of ever-changing little works . . . based in prayer . . . beginning within ourselves and our home . . . accomplished in a realistic manner . . . patiently and with perseverance . . . by simple servants . . . in response to a call, not as an escape . . . all done together in the Lord's name . . . in service to and with the support of his people." How different from my first definition!

Phil was the same Phil I had known and loved before ordination; the laying on of hands had not made him the super deacon I had once envisioned. No large letter "S" had magically appeared on his white alb when he was ordained or at any time thereafter. There was no flowing cape to suggest a super hero poised for action. Phil had simply had a stole placed over his shoulder and draped across his chest by me, his helpmate, and a brother deacon who had already experienced the joy and suffering of ordained ministry. Phil's stoles were not status symbols; they were simply a sign of the loving, caring commitment he had made to serve the Lord and his people. The stoles I had made by hand were a sign of my love and caring, too. They were stoles on loan, for after Phil's death they would eventually be passed on to his brother deacons. They were stoles on loan for many lifetimes.

14

Ministry Without End

It was only after Phil's death had freed his stoles to be passed on to other deacons that I was able to reach three additional, important conclusions about ministry. The first new discovery was that no one who ministers is indispensable. Although Phil no longer actively ministers at Holy Family, our parish still has seven liturgies complete with homilies every Sunday, and marriage and family programs are now directed by two other deacons. The shut-ins continue to receive Communion every Sunday from lay volunteers, and our Christian Family Movement groups continue to meet regularly. Furthermore, anytime one of our bishops requests a deacon to assist him at a liturgy, someone is always available.

I do not mean to imply that my husband's presence is not missed. That is not the case, but the fact remains, Phil was not *essential* to the running of any program or event at our parish, within C.F.M., or on the diocesan level. They all go on without him.

The second discovery I have made is that Phil's ministry has not ended. The story of a healing of arthritis and tales of additional "miracles" for which there is no real proof other than the proof of the heart continue to unfold. It is no wonder some people are now affectionately calling my spouse "St. Philip of Parma." Whether or not Phil will be canonized is not really important. What is important is that his ministry continues.

It is not simply through my husband's intercession that his service lives on; his ministry continues in the lives of those whom he touched. When I think of Phil's existence here on earth as being like a pebble cast into a pond, my theory comes alive. I believe Phil's existence was like a pebble cast into the pond of life, and his ministry continues to create ripples for the simple reason that many of those whom he touched continue to reach out to others who in turn reach out further still. This is creating ministry ripples—ripples which could conceivably continue to reach out to others for all time.

It is only logical that my husband's life would have created the strongest ripples in the lives of those who were closest to him. The fact that Phil's faith lives on and is being passed on by his children is evident in one teacher's comment. "There is present within your child an unusual faith element. The depth of what your child has experienced and is able to relate is a real witness to the rest of the class." Whether it involves serving at the altar, becoming a member of a school service organization, helping a friend with algebra, or teaching someone how to dribble a basketball, service has become a part of our children's lives. Was not this what Phil and I had hoped for all along—a faith so deeply rooted in each of our children that it would take the form of ministry which would be a part of them in the same way in which it was a part of us?

There is much evidence that Phil's faith-filled life has affected me, too. "Your husband's ministry is not dead. It continues in you," I have heard time and time again. Ministry has become a part of the bloodstream of my life. It has become so much a part of me and all I do that it remains one with me and I remain one with it. Yet my service of listening and sharing my life and my faith, whether with my children, another person, or a group, is different from what Phil's was as a deacon.

The basis of ministry remains constant, however. Service continues to be based in prayer and begins at home and in my writing before it reaches out to others. Because I am needed at home more than ever before and my writing takes much time, I often find myself continuing to pass up tempting ministry morsels. Family, work, and then ministry—the familiar sequence of words runs through my mind. It is so simple to say, so hard to live by.

Because the desire to minister remains so strong, I am convinced that once a woman has shared in her husband's ordination, she will always share in it. Whether she is a deacon's wife or his widow makes no difference. She shares in his ordination while he is living, and she will continue to share in the graces of his ordination after his death. Many deacons' widows will continue in the service their husbands were ordained to perform for the Church and for the People of God.

The ministry begun by my deacon husband continues, for those whom he touched in his gentle way have, in turn, continued to reach out and to touch still other people. Ripples in the pond of life, ripples begun by Phil's life and his death, extend, entwine, reach out until they are no longer visible to the naked eye.

The third thing I have learned about service in the Lord's name is that it is much more basic than I had previously thought it to be.

"Oh, Mrs. Mraz!" the lady at the neighborhood dry cleaners exclaimed. "Your husband! When he was at the altar, there was something so special about the Mass." Although I did not remember having seen this woman before, here she was telling me that it was Phil's presence at the altar, not his little works, that she remembered.

"The way Phil lived on the job preached in a way that made people think," one of his electrician friends told me.

But I had thought preaching was standing before a congregation at Mass and relating the readings to daily life.

"Dad taught me so much!" one of our children remarked. Taught? The only classes Phil had prepared were for the parish's school of religion and for expectant parents. Phil had never given lessons. Or had he? Perhaps the most valuable lesson he had taught was the example of the way he lived his life.

"If we are not able to minister in any other way, we can always minister by our example," I had told Phil when his cancer had been diagnosed. What I had not realized at the time was that my husband's greatest ministry had always been a ministry of example, a ministry of *being* so powerful that it reached out to others who never knew him.

"The person who has influenced my life the most is Deacon Phil Mraz," wrote twelve-year-old Cheri Talerico in a letter nominating my husband as the outstanding clergy or religious for the year in our diocese's annual vocation contest sponsored by the *Catholic Universe Bulletin*. Cheri wrote:

> I have cancer and Phil also had cancer. . . . When I found out I had leukemia I was so scared, I just wanted to die. When Phil found out [he had cancer] his faith just grew stronger by the day. . . . Knowing about Phil's faith makes me have a stronger faith. . . . Phil may have died, but the faith he gave me still lives on.*

Cheri and Phil had never met, had never even spoken on the phone, yet through his example related to her by others, my husband had touched her in some unexplainable way. Cheri died nearly three years after Phil, but through the example of her faith-filled life, Cheri, too, touched many people in whom her faith now lives.

"Example" is such a simple word. Ministry by example is ministry in such a simple form. "What you *are* is the diaconate, not what you are doing in ministry," a priest once shared. "The ministry and the minister are one."

*November 12, 1982, p. 8.

Gentle, concerned, sensitive, compassionate, imperfect, yet peaceful, Phil's most effective ministry had always been a ministry of being—an example for those who knew him while he walked the earth and, ultimately, an example for those who know of him merely because he had walked the earth in the best way he could while following in the footsteps of the gentle, sensitive, compassionate carpenter's son from Galilee. ''Receive the Gospel of Christ, whose herald you are. Believe what you read, teach what you believe, and practice what you teach,'' the bishop had instructed at ordination.

It has taken much time to discover what I now consider to be the essence of service in the Lord's name. Now, ministry for anyone, ordained or lay, is becoming all that God is calling us to be from the moment of conception through all eternity.

Becoming has been painful at times. It has sometimes involved numerous adjustments in thoughts and actions, extra work, stress, and emotional struggles. At Phil's ordination I had wondered at the bishop's words cautioning the men that their ministries would be accompanied by suffering. ''But likewise, be convinced that your sufferings will be fruitful, that you serve most effectively when you join your suffering with the Lord Jesus,'' the bishop had said. Our sufferings themselves are a form of ministry, and there is a joy in knowing that. Moreover, all of the sufferings which I have endured have caused a tremendous amount of personal growth within me. They have helped me to learn to be flexible in my life-style and to live fairly, if not completely, peacefully with being Deacon Phil's wife and widow. Amazingly, this has led to a sense of joy beyond belief, for I know that slowly but surely I am becoming more and more the woman God is calling me to be.

How often I have asked myself, ''If I could go back and live my life all over again, would I change anything?'' The answer is always the same—a resounding ''No, not a thing!'' I know all I have lived has been right for me. I would not change a thing, and before Phil died he said the same.

But what of life now? Already the present has called for some major, often painful, adjustments; no doubt, the future will do the same. I have had to let go of my husband and of our marriage. Replacing my dreams for the future as the deacon's wife are new dreams for me as the deacon's widow. I still hope to raise five happy, well-adjusted, loving, faith-filled children who will continue what God has begun in their lives through Phil and through me. But I dream of doing it alone here on earth with Phil's full heavenly support.

The words ''Before I formed you in the womb I knew you/before you were born I dedicated you . . .'' (Jer 1:5) are just as appropriate for me today as they were when I listened to them at Phil's ordination. But my vision of someday serving with Phil has been replaced by the hope of doing the Lord's will in my life, whatever that will may be. I look forward to Phil's ministry continuing through me as I continue to become all that I am called to be. My ministry, Phil's ministry, separate and combined, our ministry alive and well, now and for all eternity.

Once I pictured God watching me from his heavenly home while I struggled along here on earth. That vision, too, has changed. My Father is no longer confined to heaven; he walks with me daily, guiding and directing my life and gently preparing me for all that is to come. The Lord is my companion and best friend as well as my constant source of strength and support.

There is one final dream—the dream of someday meeting my heavenly Father and being reunited with Phil and the others who have gone before me. There is no better way for me to patiently await the realization of that dream than to live by the words concluding one of the bishop's prayers at Phil's ordination, the prayer consecrating the men to lives of service. This prayer is appropriate not only for me, but for all women who are deacons' wives as well:

Let them excel in every virtue: in sincere love, in the use of authority with moderation, in concern for the sick and the poor, in purity and irreproachable conduct, and in a deeply spiritual life. Let your commandments be evident in their conduct, so that the faithful may follow their good example. Let them offer the world the witness of a clear conscience. Help them to persevere, firm and steadfast in Christ. Just as your own Son came not to be served but to give himself in service to others, may these [women] imitate him on earth and reign with him in heaven.